A-Z PLYMOUTH

G000269825

CONTENTS

REFERENCE

A Road	A374
B Road	B3240
Dual Carriageway	
One-way Street Traffic flow on A Roads is also indicated by a heavy line on the driver's left.	
Restricted Access	
Pedestrianized Road	
Track / Footpath	
Residential Walkway	
Cycleway	
Railway	Level Crossing / Station / Tunnel
Built-up Area	
Local Authority Boundary	— · — · — ·
National Park Boundary	
Posttown Boundary	
Postcode Boundary within Posttown	
Map Continuation	10 / Large Scale City Centre 5

Airport	✈
Car Park (Selected)	P
Church or Chapel	†
Fire Station	■
Hospital	H
House Numbers A & B Roads only	156 / 146
Information Centre	i
National Grid Reference	245
Park & Ride	Coypool P+🚌
Police Station	▲
Post Office	★
Toilet: without facilities for the Disabled	▽
with facilities for the Disabled	▽
Viewpoint	☀ ☀
Educational Establishment	
Hospital or Hospice	
Industrial Building	
Leisure or Recreational Facility	
Place of Interest	
Public Building	
Shopping Centre or Market	
Other Selected Buildings	

SCALE

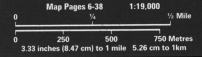

Map Pages 6-38	1:19,000
0 ¼ ½ Mile	
0 250 500 750 Metres	
3.33 inches (8.47 cm) to 1 mile	5.26 cm to 1km

Map Pages 4-5	1:9,500
0 ⅛ ¼ Mile	
0 125 250 375 Metres	
6.67 inches (16.94 cm) to 1 mile	10.52 cm to 1km

Copyright of Geographers' A-Z Map Company Limited

Fairfield Road, Borough Green, Sevenoaks, Kent TN15 8PP
Telephone: 01732 781000 (Enquiries & Trade Sales)
01732 783422 (Retail Sales)

www.a-zmaps.co.uk

Ordnance Survey® This product includes mapping data licensed from Ordnance Survey® with the permission of the Controller of Her Majesty's Stationery Office.

© Crown Copyright 2005. All rights reserved. License number 100017302

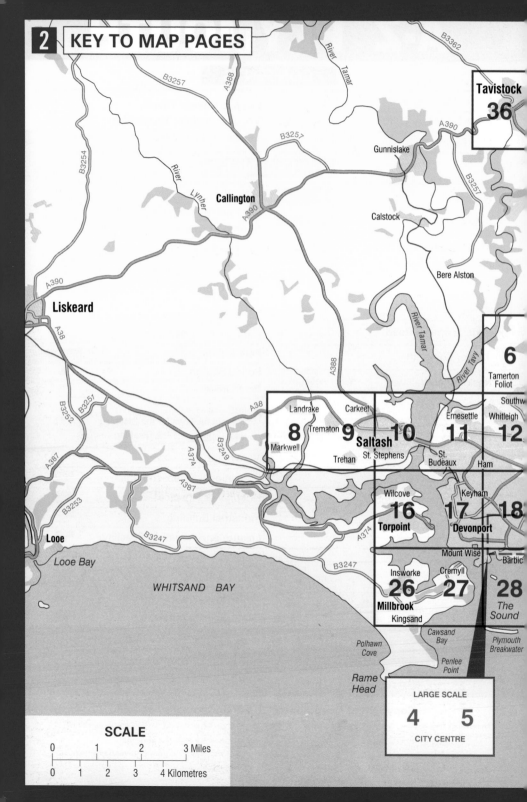

2 **KEY TO MAP PAGES**

Tavistock
36

Liskeard

Callington

Gunnislake

Calstock

Bere Alston

6
Tamerton
Foliot

Landrake   Carkeel
8   Trematon   **9**   **10**   **11**   **12**
Markwell   Saltash   Ernesettle   Whitleigh   Southw
Trehan   St. Stephens   St.   Ham
Budeaux

Wilcove   Keyham
16   **17**   **18**
Torpoint   Devonport

Mount Wise   Barbic

Insworke   Cremyll
26   **27**   **28**
Millbrook   The
Kingsand   Sound

Looe

Looe Bay

WHITSAND   BAY

Polhawn
Cove

Cawsand
Bay

Plymouth
Breakwater

Penlee
Point

Rame
Head

LARGE SCALE
4   **5**
CITY CENTRE

SCALE
0   1   2   3 Miles
0   1   2   3   4 Kilometres

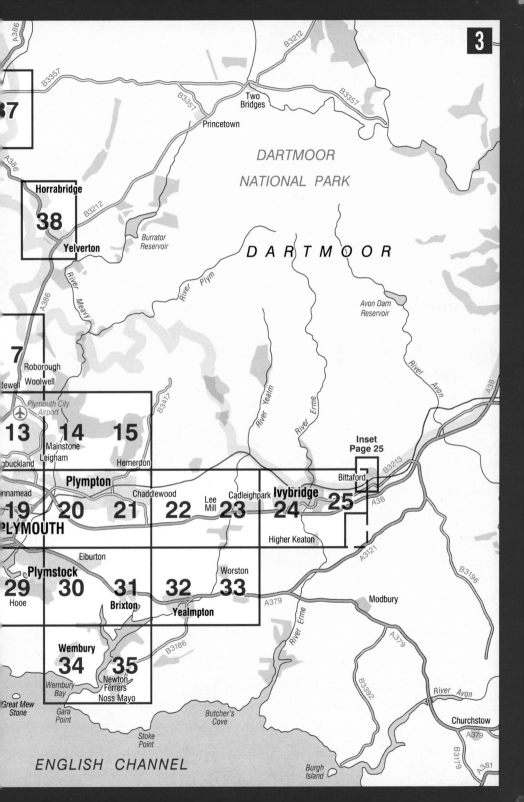

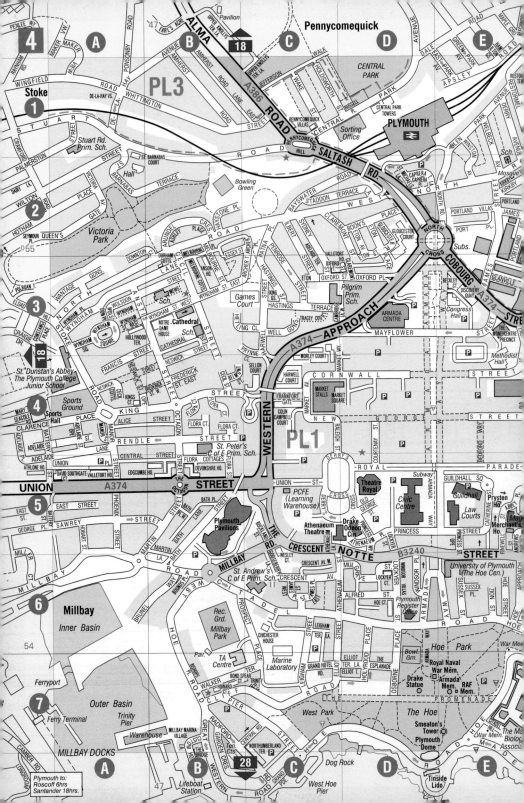

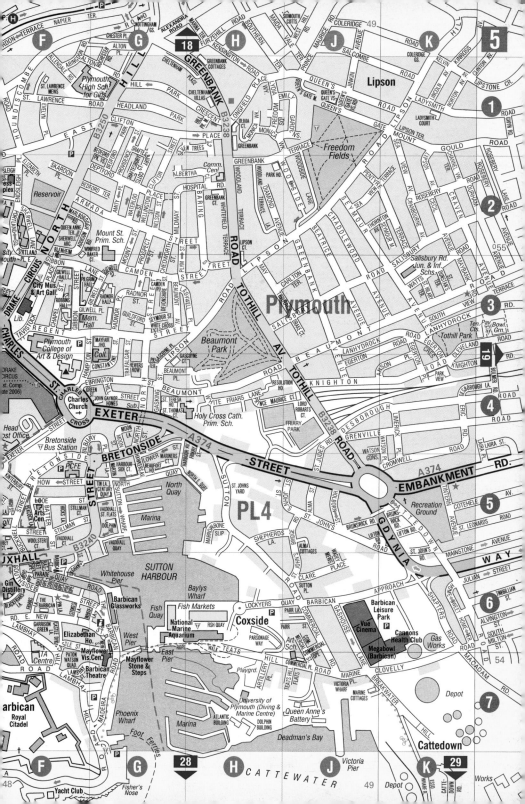

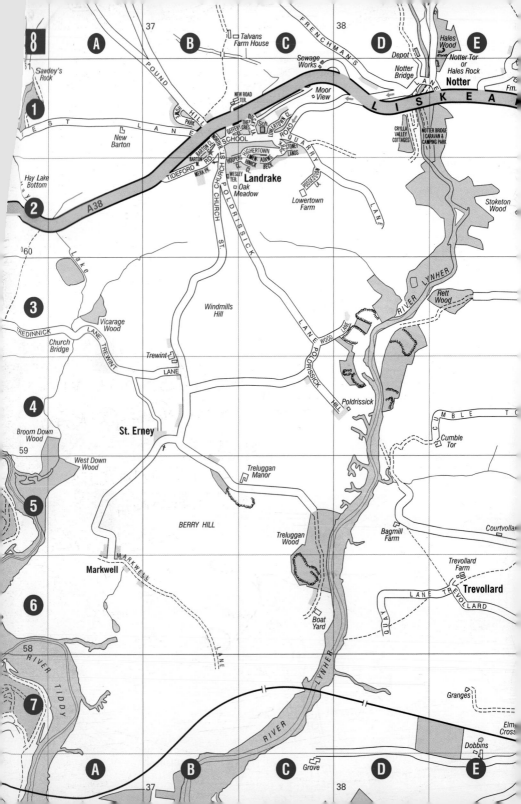

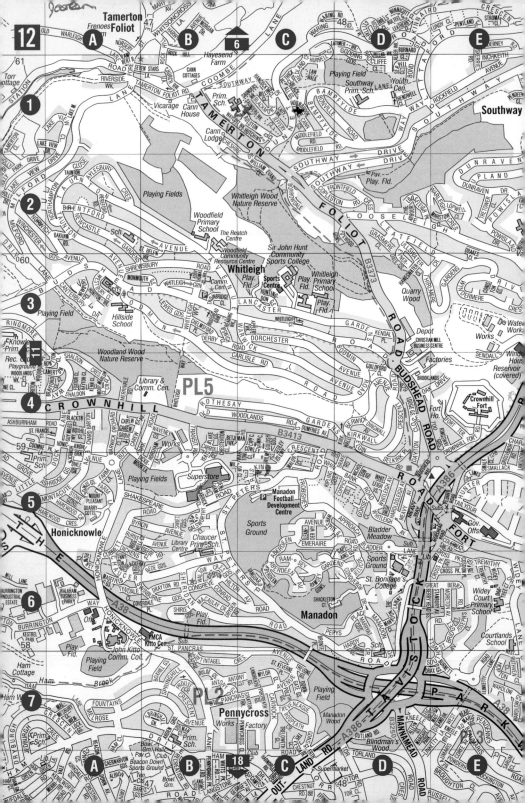

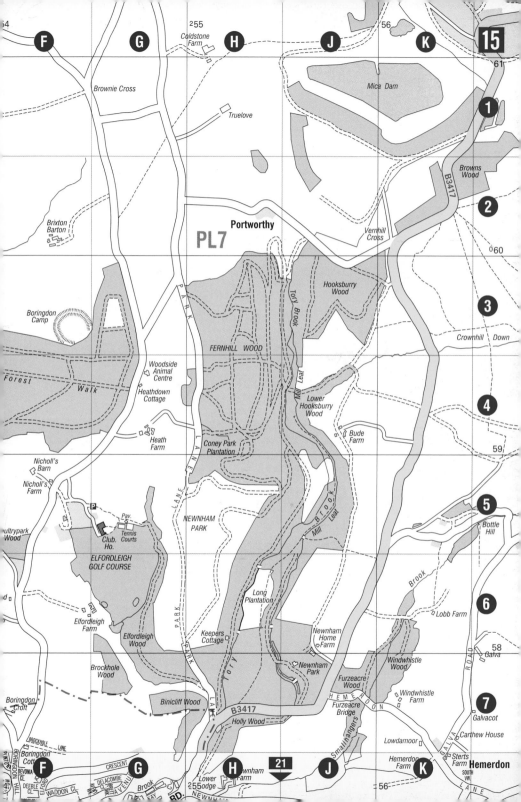

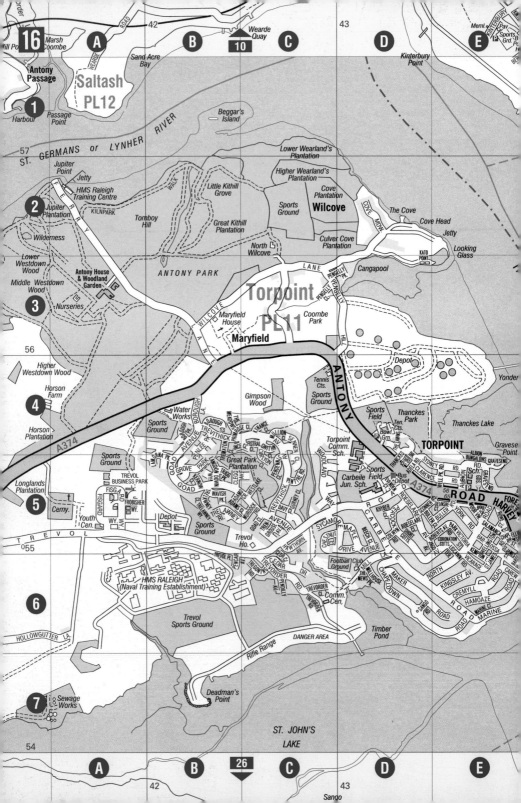

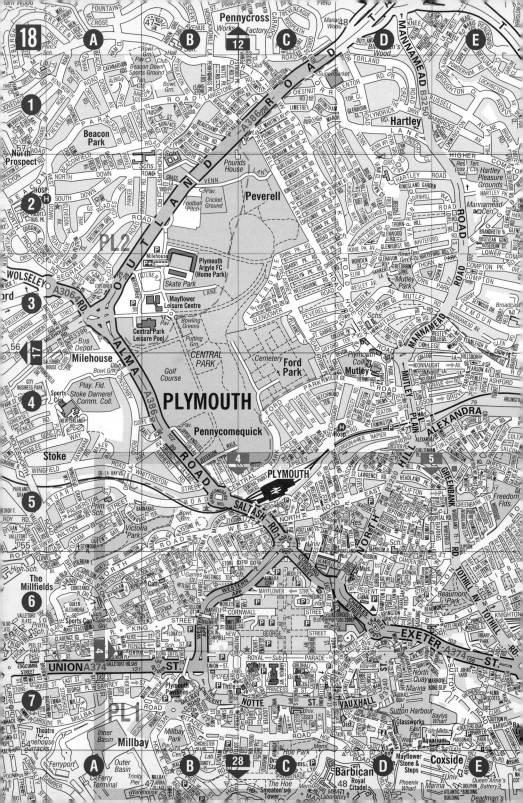

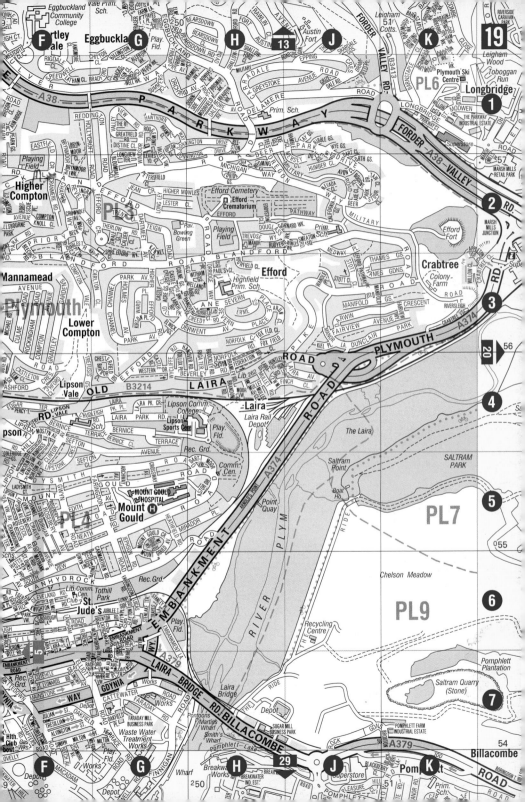

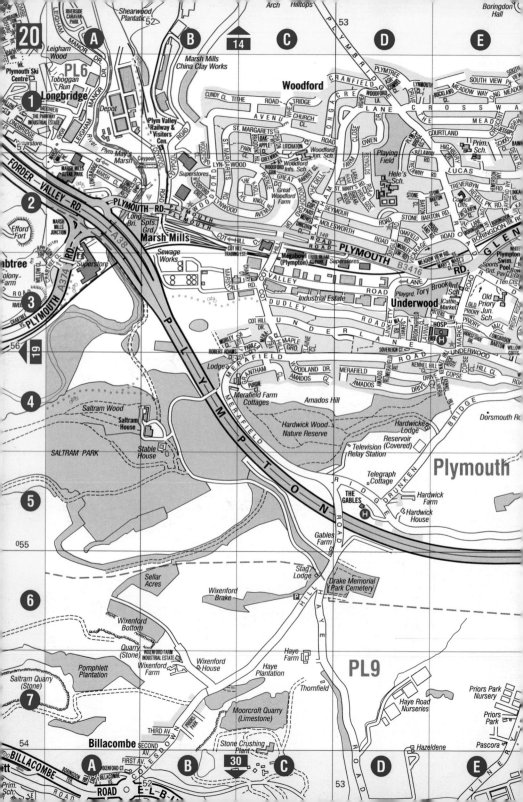

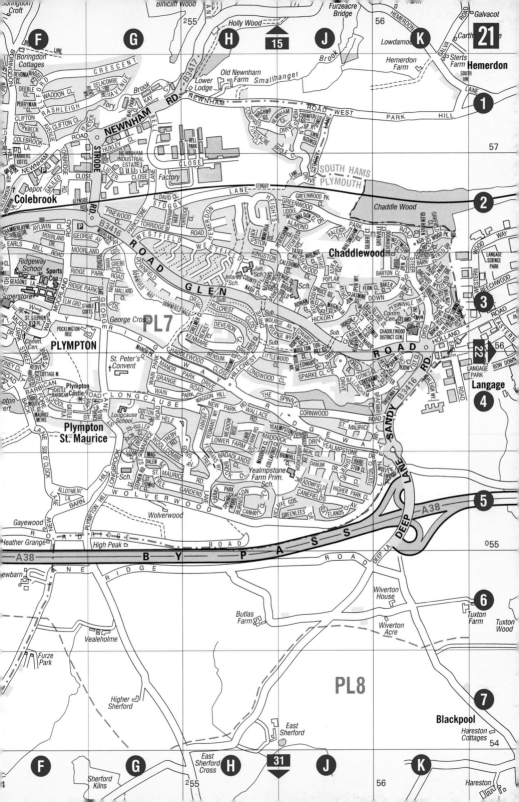

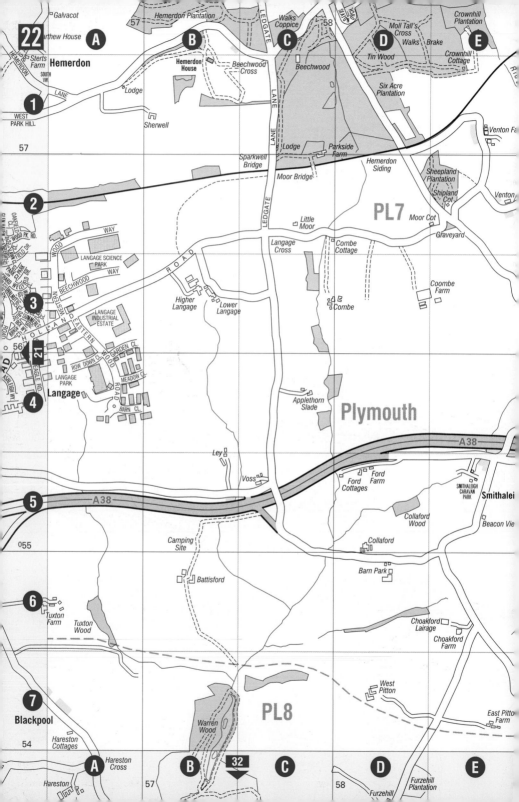

F · G · H · J · K

4

RIVER TAMAR

H M DOCKYARD SOUTH 245

Prim. Sch.

SEYMOUR Ho.
Scott Mem.

17

J

Pav.
Ten. Cts.
Admiralty Ho.

46

Stonehall Works

Stonehall FLATS

Stonehouse Barracks

Theatre

27

Richmond
HAMOAZE

Mutton Cove Pier

Mount Wise Outdoor Pools

Mount Wise Hard

Mount Wise

RICHMOND ST

OCEAN

Mayflower International Marina

54

Ferryport

1

PLYMOUTH CARADON

Cremyll to Plymouth Foot Ferry

Pontoons

Ocean Quay

Quarterdeck

POUND

Telegraph Wharf

Freeman's Wharf

William St

ROAD

Sports Grd.
Prim. Sch.

Shipyard

Cremyll

The Narrows

BREWHOUSE

CLARENCE

ROYAL WILLIAM YD

Admiralty Cotts

Playgrd.

2

Works

B3247

The Avenue

Devil's Point

Firestone Bay

East

Mount Edgcumbe Formal Gardens

Wilderness Point

Western King Point

53

Empacombe

Barnpool Wood

Barn Pool

Sheep Park

Beech Wood

3

Palmer Rock

Garden Cottage

Cricket Grd.

Mount Edgcumbe Ho.

Lower Walk

Palmer Point

No.6 Redoubt

Mount Edgcumbe Farm

Barrow Park

Higher Walk

Dry Walk

MOUNT EDGCUMBE COUNTRY PARK

The Raven's Cliffs

28 ▶

Nanny Parson's Grove

Lower Deerhouse Plantation

Amphitheatre Wood

Ravenness Point

Pigshill Wood

Drywalk Wood

Harbour View Plantation

Oak Plantation

The Bridge

4

LOWER ANDERTON

Deer Park

Lady Emma's Cottage

052

Maker Farm

Grave Yard

Maker Lodge

Grotton Plantation

Warren Plantation

Inner Redding

O E

Picklecombe Seat

Redding Point Plantation

Red Seat

Redding Point

5

Hooe Lake Valley

The Earthquake

South Terrace

LAKE

Hooe Lake Cott.

Fort Picklecombe

Picklecombe Point

Warn Sandway

Hooe Lake Point

Cawsand to Plymouth (Barbican) Foot Ferry (Summer Only)

6

51

Sandway Point

7

CAWSAND BAY

Lighthouse

Millbay

A Inner Basin

B

18

C

D

E Coxside

1

Millbay Docks

PLYMOUTH

Barbican

2

Firestone Bay

53

Drake's Island

3

Plymouth (Barbican)
(Summer Only) to Cawsand
Foot Ferry

Mount Batten
Breakwater

Mount Batten
Point

27

Batten Bay

Dunstone
Point

Rum Bay

4

THE SOUND

052

Jer

5

Wyatt's
Way

Ramscliff Point

Rams
Cliff

Staddon
Cottage

6

Plymouth to:
Roscoff 6hrs.
Santander 18hrs

Leekbed Bay

51

Bovisand Pier

Diving Disease
Research Centre

7

Staddon Point

Bovisand
Fort

Lighthouse

Signal
Station

Breakwater
Fort

Pier

A

B Plymouth Breakwater

C

D

E Bov

47

48

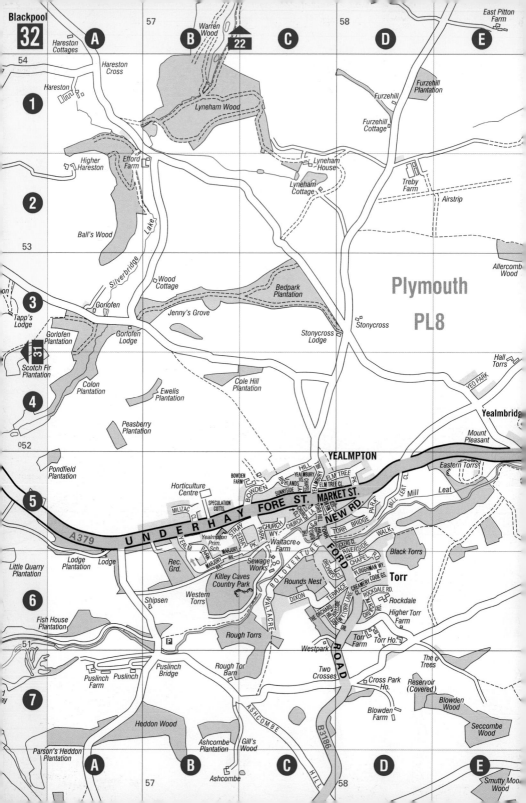

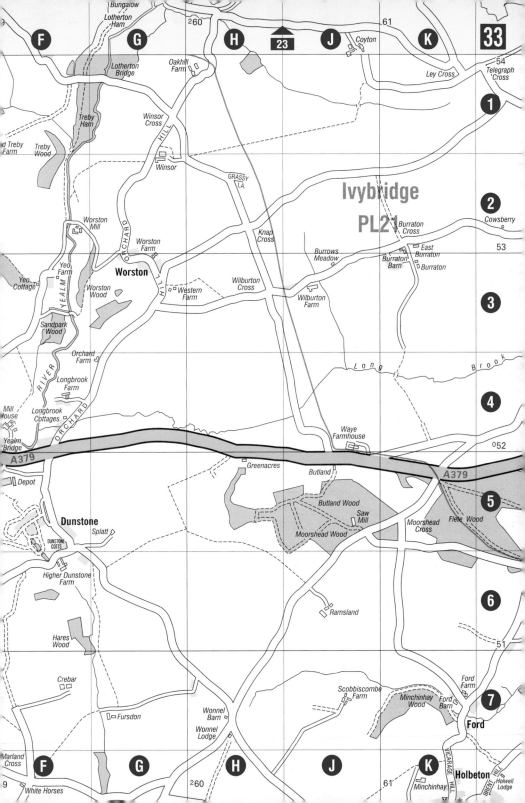

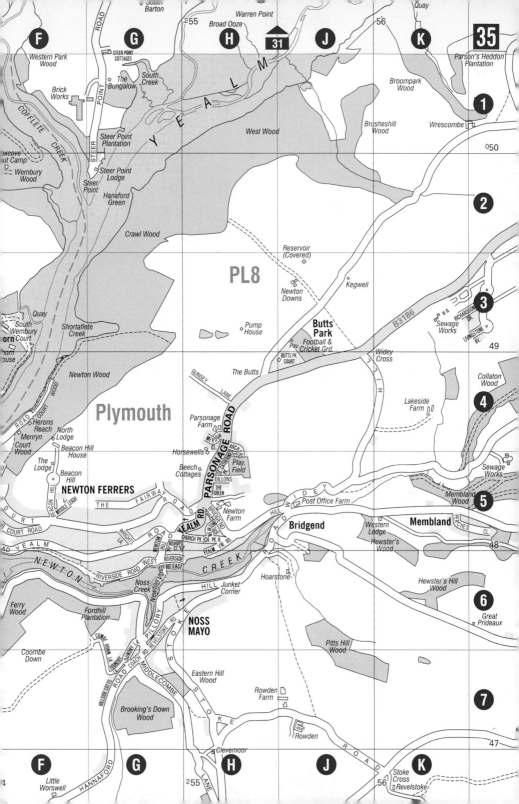

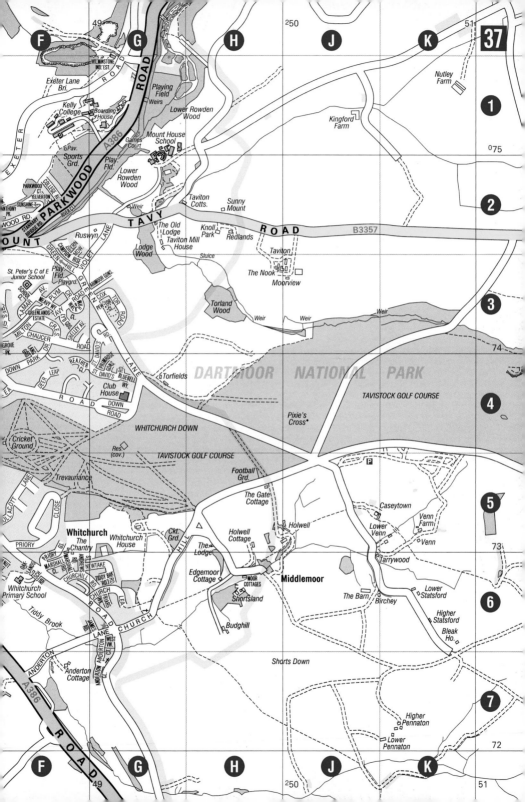

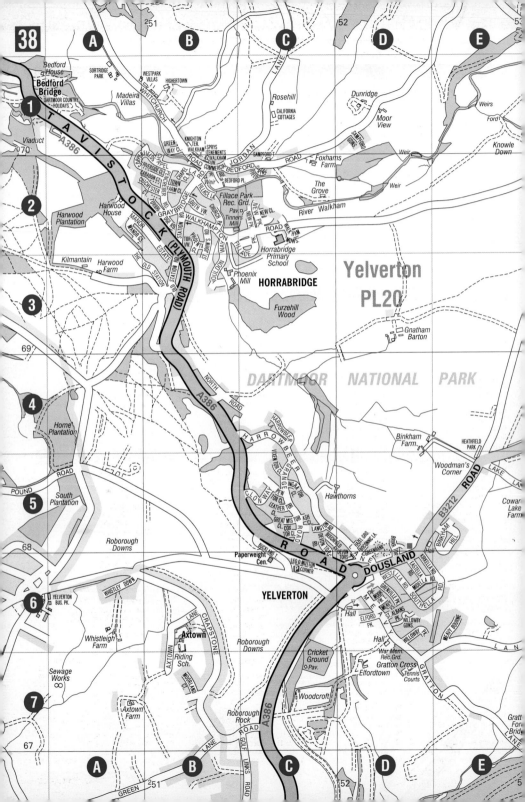

INDEX

Including Streets, Places & Areas, Hospitals & Hospices, Industrial Estates,
Selected Flats & Walkways, Stations, and Selected Places of Interest.

HOW TO USE THIS INDEX

1. Each street name is followed by its Postcode District and then by its Locality abbreviation(s) and then by its map reference;
e.g. **Abbey Ct.** PL1: Ply . . . .5F **5** is in the PL1 Postcode District and the Plymouth Locality and is to be found in square 5F on page **5**. The page number is shown in bold type.

2. A strict alphabetical order is followed in which Av., Rd., St., etc. (though abbreviated) are read in full and as part of the street name; e.g. **Abbeymead M.** appears after **Abbey Ct.** but before **Abbey Pl.**

3. Streets and a selection of flats and walkways too small to be shown on the maps, appear in the index with the thoroughfare to which it is connected shown in brackets; e.g. **Albion Ct.** PL11: Torp . . . .5E **16** (off Albion Rd.)

4. Addresses that are in more than one part are referred to as not continuous.

5. Places and areas are shown in the index in **BLUE TYPE** and the map reference is to the actual map square in which the town centre or area is located and not to the place name shown on the map; e.g. **ANDERTON** 4C **26**

6. An example of a selected place of interest is Tavistock Mus. 3E **36**

7. An example of a station is **Devonport Station (Rail)** 5J **17**

8. An example of a hospital is DERRIFORD HOSPITAL 3G **13**

9. Map references for entries that appear on large scale pages **4-5** are shown first, with small scale map references shown in brackets; e.g. **Abbey Pl.** PL1: Ply 5E **4** (7C **18**)

GENERAL ABBREVIATIONS

App. : Approach	**Dr.** : Drive	**La.** : Lane	**Rd.** : Road
Arc. : Arcade	**E.** : East	**Lit.** : Little	**Sth.** : South
Av. : Avenue	**Est.** : Estate	**Lwr.** : Lower	**Sq.** : Square
Bri. : Bridge	**Fld.** : Field	**Mnr.** : Manor	**St.** : Street
Bldg. : Building	**Gdn.** : Garden	**Mkt.** : Market	**Ter.** : Terrace
Bldgs. : Buildings	**Gdns.** : Gardens	**Mdw.** : Meadow	**Trad.** : Trading
Bus. : Business	**Ga.** : Gate	**Mdws.** : Meadows	**Up.** : Upper
Cvn. : Caravan	**Gt.** : Great	**M.** : Mews	**Va.** : Vale
Cen. : Centre	**Grn.** : Green	**Mt.** : Mount	**Vw.** : View
Cir. : Circus	**Gro.** : Grove	**Mus.** : Museum	**Vs.** : Villas
Cl. : Close	**Hgts.** : Heights	**Nth.** : North	**Vis.** : Visitors
Cnr. : Corner	**Ho.** : House	**Pde.** : Parade	**Wlk.** : Walk
Cotts. : Cottages	**Ind.** : Industrial	**Pk.** : Park	**W.** : West
Ct. : Court	**Info.** : Information	**Pl.** : Place	**Yd.** : Yard
Cres. : Crescent	**Intl.** : International	**Quad.** : Quadrant	
Cft. : Croft	**Junc.** : Junction	**Ri.** : Rise	

LOCALITY ABBREVIATIONS

B Fer : **Bere Ferrers**	Erm : **Ermington**	N Fer : **Newton Ferrers**	T Fol : **Tamerton Foliot**
Bit : **Bittaford**	Filh : **Filham**	N May : **Noss Mayo**	Tav : **Tavistock**
Bov : **Bovisand**	Har : **Harford**	Nott : **Notter**	Torp : **Torpoint**
Brix : **Brixton**	Hem : **Hemerdon**	Ply : **Plymouth**	Torr : **Torr**
B Mon : **Buckland Monachorum**	Holb : **Holbeton**	P'ton : **Plympton**	T'han : **Trehan**
Car : **Carkeel**	Hoo : **Hooe**	P'ock : **Plymstock**	Trem : **Trematon**
C'one : **Crapstone**	Hor : **Horrabridge**	Rob : **Roborough**	Trew : **Trewetha**
Crem : **Cremyll**	Ivy : **Ivybridge**	S Ern : **St Erney**	Wem : **Wembury**
Dev : **Devonport**	Kin : **Kingsand**	Salt : **Saltash**	Whit : **Whitchurch**
Dous : **Dousland**	Lan : **Landrake**	Smi : **Smithaleigh**	Wil : **Wilcove**
D Tho : **Down Thomas**	L Mil : **Lee Mill**	S'ell : **Sparkwell**	Wors : **Worston**
Duns : **Dunstone**	Mem : **Membland**	Spr : **Spriddlestone**	Yeal : **Yealmpton**
Elb : **Elburton**	Mill : **Millbrook**	Stad : **Staddiscombe**	Yel : **Yelverton**

A

Abbey Ct. PL1: Ply 5F **5**
Abbeymead M. PL19: Tav 3E **36**
Abbey Pl. PL1: Ply 5E **4** (7C **18**)
    PL19: Tav 2D **36**
    (Bannawell St.)
    PL19: Tav 3E **36**
    (Dolvin Rd.)
Abbey Ri. PL19: Tav 3E **36**
Abbot Rd. PL21: Ivy 2B **24**
Abbotsbury Way PL2: Ply 7J **11**
Abbots Cl. PL21: L Mil 4K **23**
Abbotsfield Cl. PL19: Tav 4B **36**
Abbotsfield Cres. PL19: Tav . . .4B **36**
Abbotts Rd. PL3: Ply 3D **18**
Aberdeen Av. PL5: Ply 6C **12**
Abingdon Rd.
    PL4: Ply 1F **5** (5D **18**)

Abney Cres. PL6: Ply 1G **13**
Acklington Pl. PL5: Ply 3H **11**
Acland Rd. PL21: Ivy 2B **24**
Acre Cotts. PL1: Dev 5J **17**
Acre Pl. PL1: Dev 5J **17**
Adams Beck PL12: Lan 2C **8**
Adams Cl. PL5: Ply 6H **11**
    PL11: Torp 5B **16**
Adams Cres. PL11: Torp 5B **16**
Adam's La. PL9: D Tho 2A **34**
Addison Rd. PL4: Ply . .2F **5** (5D **18**)
Adelaide La.
    PL1: Ply 5A **4** (7A **18**)
Adelaide Pl.
    PL1: Ply 4A **4** (6A **18**)
Adelaide St.
    PL1: Ply 4A **4** (6A **18**)
    PL2: Ply 3J **17**
Adelaide St. Ope
    PL1: Ply 4A **4** (6A **18**)

Adelaide Ter. PL1: Ply 2C **4**
Adela Rd. PL11: Torp 5D **16**
Adit La. PL12: Salt 4B **10**
Admiral's Hard PL1: Ply 1K **27**
Admiralty Cotts. PL1: Dev 2K **27**
Admiralty Ope Nth.
    PL2: Ply 2H **17**
Admiralty Ope Sth.
    PL2: Ply 2H **17**
Admiralty Rd. PL1: Ply 1K **27**
    PL5: Ply 5F **11**
Admiralty St. PL1: Ply 1K **27**
    PL2: Ply 2H **17**
Agaton Fort Rd. PL5: Ply 4J **11**
Agaton Rd. PL5: Ply 5H **11**
Ainslie Ter. PL2: Ply 1H **17**
Aire Gdns. PL3: Ply 3H **19**
Alamein Ct. PL12: Salt 5A **10**
Alamein Rd. PL12: Salt 5A **10**
Albany St. PL1: Dev 6H **17**

Albemarle Vs. PL1: Ply 5J **17**
Albertha Cl. PL4: Ply . .2G **5** (5E **18**)
Albert Rd. PL2: Dev 5H **17**
    PL12: Salt 5C **10**
Albion Bungalows
    PL11: Torp 5E **16**
Albion Ct. PL11: Torp 5E **16**
    (off Albion Rd.)
Albion Dr. PL2: Ply 1A **18**
Albion Rd. PL11: Torp 5E **16**
Alcester Cl. PL2: Dev 4H **17**
Alcester St. PL2: Dev 4J **17**
Alden Wlk. PL6: Ply 1G **19**
Alder Rd. PL19: Tav 5E **36**
Alderney Rd. PL6: Ply 7E **6**
Aldersley Wlk. PL6: Ply 7F **13**
Alexandra Cl. PL9: Elb 1C **30**
Alexandra Rd. PL4: Ply 4D **18**
    PL10: Mill 4B **26**
    (off Blindwell Hill)

Benbow St.—California Cotts.

Benbow St. PL2: Dev . . . 4J **17**
Bennets La. PL12: Salt . . . 4C **10**
Bennett St. PL1: Dev . . . 7H **17**
Beresford St. PL2: Ply . . . 4K **17**
Berkeley Cotts. PL1: Ply . . . 5K **17**
Berkeley Way PL21: Ivy . . . 4E **24**
Berkshire Dr. PL2: Ply . . . 3J **17**
Bernice Cl. PL4: Ply . . . 4G **19**
Bernice Ter. PL4: Ply . . . 4F **19**
Berrow Pk. Rd. PL3: Ply . . . 1C **18**
Berry Head Gdns. PL6: Ply . . . 6D **12**
Berry Pk. PL12: Salt . . . 3A **10**
Berry Pk. Cl. PL9: P'ock . . . 3K **29**
Berry Pk. Rd. PL9: P'ock . . . 2K **29**
Berthon Rd. PL5: Ply . . . 1E **16**
Berwick Av. PL5: Ply . . . 4D **12**
Betjeman Wlk. PL5: Ply . . . 4B **12**
Beverley Rd. PL3: Ply . . . 4H **19**
Beverston Way PL6: Ply . . . 6G **7**
Beweys Pk. PL12: Salt . . . 5K **9**
Beyrout Cotts. *PL1: Dev . . . 5J 17*
(off Beyrout Pl.)
Beyrout Pl. PL1: Dev . . . 5J **17**
Bickern Rd. PL11: Torp . . . 5E **16**
Bickham Pk. Rd. PL3: Ply . . . 2C **18**
Bickham Rd. PL5: Ply . . . 5G **11**
Bickleigh Cl. PL6: Ply . . . 6F **13**
Bickleigh Down Bus. Pk.
PL6: Ply . . . 6J **7**
Bickleigh Down Rd.
PL6: Rob . . . 6H **7**
Bicton Cl. PL6: Ply . . . 6J **13**
Biddick Dr. PL2: Ply . . . 2J **17**
Bideford Wlk. PL6: Ply . . . 7K **13**
Bigbury Wlk. PL6: Ply . . . 7K **13**
Biggin Hill PL5: Ply . . . 2J **11**
Bilbury St. PL4: Ply . . . 4F **5** (6D **18**)
BILLACOMBE . . . 1A 30
Billacombe Rd. PL9: P'ock . . . 7H **19**
Billacombe Vs. PL9: P'ock . . . 1A **30**
Billing Cl. PL6: Ply . . . 1C **12**
Billington Cl. PL6: Ply . . . 7G **13**
Binkham Hill PL20: Yel . . . 5E **38**
Bircham Vw. PL6: Ply . . . 6H **13**
Birch Cl. PL6: Ply . . . 7K **7**
Birches, The PL6: Ply . . . 1J **13**
Birchfield Av. PL2: Ply . . . 2A **18**
Birch Pond Rd. PL9: P'ock . . . 2J **29**
Birchwood Cl. PL19: Tav . . . 5E **36**
Birchwood Gdns.
PL7: P'ton . . . 1H **21**
Birkbeck Cl. PL7: P'ton . . . 1F **21**
Birkdale Cl. PL12: Salt . . . 5K **9**
Biscombe Gdns. PL12: Salt . . . 4D **10**
Bishops Cl. PL12: Salt . . . 4B **10**
PL21: Ivy . . . 2F **25**
Bishops Ct. PL8: N Fer . . . 5G **35**
Bishops Pl. PL1: Ply . . . 7B **4** (1B **28**)
BITTAFORD . . . 6K 25
Bittaford Ter. PL21: Bit . . . 7K **25**
Bittaford Wood PL21: Bit . . . 7K **25**
Bittaford Wood Pk. Homes
PL21: Bit . . . 7K **25**
Blachford Rd. PL21: Ivy . . . 2C **24**
Blackall Gdns. PL6: Ply . . . 1C **12**
Blackberry Cl. PL9: P'ock . . . 1J **29**
Blackberry La. PL9: P'ock . . . 1K **29**
Blackett Cl. PL21: Ivy . . . 3F **25**
Blackeven Cl. PL6: Rob . . . 5J **7**
Blackeven Hill PL6: Rob . . . 5J **7**
Blackfriars La. PL1: Ply . . . 6F **5**
Blackfriars Ope PL1: Ply . . . 6F **5**
Blackmore Cres. PL6: Ply . . . 1C **12**
BLACKPOOL . . . 7K 21
Blackstone Cl. PL9: Elb . . . 3C **30**
Blackthorn Cl. PL5: Ply . . . 4A **12**
PL6: Ply . . . 6J **7**
Blackthorn Dr. PL21: Ivy . . . 4F **25**
Bladder La. PL5: Ply . . . 5D **12**
Blairgowrie Rd. PL5: Ply . . . 5F **11**
Blair Rd. PL21: Ivy . . . 4E **24**
Blake Gdns. PL5: Ply . . . 4B **12**
Blanchard Pl. PL7: P'ton . . . 1F **21**
Blandford Rd. PL3: Ply . . . 3F **19**
Blaxton La. PL5: T Fol . . . 3A **6**
Blenheim Rd.
PL4: Ply . . . 2F **5** (5D **18**)
Blindwell Hill PL10: Mill . . . 4B **26**
Blindwell Ter. PL10: Mill . . . 4B **26**
Bloomball Cl. PL3: Ply . . . 2G **19**
Blubell Cl. PL12: Salt . . . 3A **10**
Bluebell Way PL19: Tav . . . 4G **37**
Blue Haze Cl. PL6: Ply . . . 2J **13**
Blunts La. PL6: Ply . . . 3H **13**
Boconnic La. PL20: Yel . . . 5D **38**
Bodmin Rd. PL5: Ply . . . 3A **12**
Boldventure PL8: Torr . . . 6C **32**
Bolt Ho. Cl. PL19: Tav . . . 3C **36**
Bond Spear Ct. PL1: Ply . . . 7B **4**
Bond St. PL6: Ply . . . 1D **12**
Bonville Rd. PL6: Ply . . . 1C **12**
Boon's Pl. PL1: Ply . . . 2D **4** (5C **18**)
Boringdon Camp . . . 3F 15
Boringdon Cl. PL7: P'ton . . . 1E **20**
Boringdon Hill PL7: P'ton . . . 1F **21**
Boringdon Pk. PL21: Ivy . . . 3B **24**
Boringdon Rd. PL7: P'ton . . . 2E **20**
PL9: Hoo . . . 2F **29**
Boringdon Ter. PL7: P'ton . . . 2E **20**
PL9: Hoo . . . 2F **29**
PL9: P'ock . . . 1A **30**
Boringdon Vs. PL7: P'ton . . . 2E **20**
Borough, The PL8: Yeal . . . 5C **32**
Borough Ct. PL11: Torp . . . 4B **16**
Borough La. PL11: Torp . . . 4B **16**
Borough Pk. PL11: Torp . . . 4B **16**
Borringdon Av. PL5: Ply . . . 7G **11**
Borrowdale Cl. PL6: Ply . . . 2C **12**
Boscastle Gdns. PL2: Ply . . . 7B **12**
Boscawen Pl. PL2: Dev . . . 4H **17**
Boscundle Row *PL12: Salt . . . 5D 10*
(off Albert Rd.)
Boswell Cl. PL5: Ply . . . 5A **12**
Bottle Pk. PL21: L Mil . . . 4G **23**
Boughthayes PL19: Tav . . . 3C **36**
Boughthayes Est. PL19: Tav . . . 4C **36**
Boulden Cl. PL7: P'ton . . . 3K **21**
Boulter Cl. PL6: Rob . . . 5H **7**
Bounds Pl. PL1: Ply . . . 6B **4** (7B **18**)
Bourne Cl. PL3: Ply . . . 2J **19**
Boville La. PL9: Elb . . . 2D **30**
BOVISAND . . . 7F 29
Bovisand Fort . . . 7E 28
Bovisand La.
PL9: Bov, Stad . . . 7G **29**
PL9: D Tho . . . 7H **29**
Bovisand Lodge Est.
PL9: Bov . . . 7G **29**
Bovisand Rd. PL9: Stad . . . 7J **29**
Bowden Farm PL8: Yeal . . . 5B **32**
Bowden Hill PL8: Yeal . . . 5C **32**
Bowden Pk. Rd. PL6: Ply . . . 6F **13**
Bowdens Pk. PL21: Ivy . . . 4C **24**
Bowers Pk. Dr. PL6: Ply . . . 7K **7**
Bowers Rd. PL2: Ply . . . 3A **18**
Bowhays Wlk. PL6: Ply . . . 1H **19**
Boxhill Cl. PL5: Ply . . . 4A **12**
Boxhill Gdns. PL2: Ply . . . 7B **12**
Bracken Cl. PL6: Ply . . . 6J **7**
Braddons Hill PL7: P'ton . . . 1C **20**
Bradfield Cl. PL6: Ply . . . 6K **13**
Bradford Cl. PL6: Ply . . . 1G **19**
Bradley Rd. PL4: Ply . . . 4E **18**
Braemar Cl. PL7: P'ton . . . 4K **21**
Brake Rd. PL5: Ply . . . 5D **12**
Bramble Cl. PL3: Ply . . . 1G **19**
Bramble Wlk. PL6: Ply . . . 1H **19**
Bramfield Pl. PL6: Ply . . . 1J **19**
Bramley Rd. PL3: Ply . . . 4H **19**
Brancker Rd. PL2: Ply . . . 2B **18**
Brandon Rd. PL3: Ply . . . 4H **19**
Brandreth Rd. PL3: Ply . . . 2E **18**
Branscombe Gdns. PL5: Ply . . . 4K **11**
Branson Ct. PL7: P'ton . . . 3K **21**
Braunton Wlk. PL6: Ply . . . 7K **13**
Bray Cl. PL19: Tav . . . 3C **36**
Brayford Cl. PL5: Ply . . . 4A **12**
Breakwater Hill
PL4: Ply . . . 7J **5** (1F **29**)
Breakwater Ind. Est.
PL9: P'ock . . . 1H **29**
Breakwater Rd. PL9: P'ock . . . 1H **29**
Brean Down Cl. PL3: Ply . . . 2D **18**
Brean Down Rd. PL3: Ply . . . 1D **18**
Brecon Cl. PL3: Ply . . . 1F **19**
Brentford Av. PL5: Ply . . . 2A **12**
Brent Hill PL8: Holb . . . 7K **33**
Brent Knoll Rd.
PL3: Ply . . . 2D **18**
Brentor Rd. PL4: Ply . . . 6G **19**
Brest Rd. PL6: Ply . . . 3F **13**
Brest Way PL6: Ply . . . 4F **13**
Bretonside PL4: Ply . . . 5F **5** (7D **18**)
Brett Wlk. PL7: P'ton . . . 1G **21**
Brewhouse PL1: Ply . . . 1J **27**
Briansway PL12: Salt . . . 5A **10**
Briardale Rd. PL2: Ply . . . 2J **17**
Briarleigh Cl. PL6: Ply . . . 5A **14**
Briar Rd. PL3: Ply . . . 1E **18**
Briars Wlk. PL12: Salt . . . 3A **10**
Briar Tor PL20: Yel . . . 5D **38**
Brickfields Cl. PL1: Dev . . . 6J **17**
Bridge, The PL1: Ply . . . 7B **4**
BRIDGEND . . . 5J 35
Bridgend Hill PL8: N Fer . . . 5H **35**
Bridge Pk. PL21: Ivy . . . 3E **24**
Bridges, The PL12: Salt . . . 6B **10**
Bridgwater Cl. PL6: Ply . . . 6G **13**
Bridle Cl. PL7: P'ton . . . 1J **21**
Bridle Way PL12: Salt . . . 3A **10**
Bridwell Cl. PL5: Ply . . . 7H **11**
Bridwell La. Nth. PL5: Ply . . . 7H **11**
Bridwell Rd. PL5: Ply . . . 7H **11**
Brimhill Cl. PL7: P'ton . . . 5J **21**
Brismar Wlk. PL6: Ply . . . 1H **19**
Britannia Pl. PL4: Ply . . . 6G **19**
Brixham Wlk. PL6: Ply . . . 7K **13**
BRIXTON . . . 4H 31
Brixton Lodge Gdns.
PL8: Brix . . . 4G **31**
Broadland Gdns.
PL9: P'ock . . . 1B **30**
Broadland La. PL9: P'ock . . . 1A **30**
Broadlands Cl. PL7: P'ton . . . 5H **21**
Broad La. PL12: Trem . . . 4E **8**
Broadley Ct. PL6: Rob . . . 4G **7**
Broadley Ind. Pk. PL6: Rob . . . 4G **7**
Broadley Pk. Rd. PL6: Rob . . . 5F **7**
Broad Pk. PL9: P'ock . . . 2H **29**
Broad Pk. Rd. PL3: Ply . . . 2C **18**
Broad Wlk. PL12: Salt . . . 6B **10**
Broadway, The PL9: P'ock . . . 2K **29**
Brockhole La. PL7: P'ton . . . 7F **15**
Brockley Rd. PL3: Ply . . . 4H **19**
Brockton Gdns. PL6: Ply . . . 1G **13**
Bromhead Ct. PL6: Ply . . . 7F **13**
Bromley Pl. PL2: Ply . . . 4K **17**
Bronte Pl. PL5: Ply . . . 6C **12**
Brook, The PL12: Salt . . . 3B **10**
Brook Cl. PL7: P'ton . . . 5H **21**
Brookdown Ter.
PL12: Salt . . . 4B **10**
Brookdown Vs. PL12: Salt . . . 4B **10**
Brooke Cl. PL12: Salt . . . 5D **10**
Brookfield Cl. PL7: P'ton . . . 3J **21**
Brooking Cl. PL6: Ply . . . 6F **13**
Brookingfield Cl.
PL7: P'ton . . . 3D **20**
Brooking Way PL12: Salt . . . 4K **9**
Brooklands PL6: Ply . . . 4D **12**
Brook Rd. PL21: Ivy . . . 3E **24**
Brook's Hill PL12: Salt . . . 3B **10**
Brooks La. PL10: Mill . . . 4C **26**
Brook St. PL19: Tav . . . 2E **36**
Brookwood Rd. PL9: Elb . . . 2E **30**
Broomfield Dr. PL9: Hoo . . . 3G **29**
Broom Hill PL12: Salt . . . 5A **10**
Broom Pk. PL9: Hoo . . . 4J **29**
Broughton Cl. PL3: Ply . . . 1E **18**
Brownhill La. PL9: Wem . . . 3C **34**
Browning Rd. PL2: Ply . . . 3K **17**
Brownlow St. PL1: Ply . . . 7K **17**
(not continuous)
Broxton Dr. PL9: P'ock . . . 7K **19**
Brunel Av. PL2: Ply . . . 3J **17**
Brunel Rd. PL12: Salt . . . 3K **9**
Brunel Ter. PL2: Ply . . . 3J **17**
Brunel Vw. PL12: Salt . . . 4D **10**
Brunel Way PL1: Ply . . . 6A **4** (7A **18**)
PL21: Ivy . . . 2F **25**
Brunswick Pl. PL2: Dev . . . 4J **17**
Brunswick Rd.
PL4: Ply . . . 5J **5** (7E **18**)
(not continuous)
Brynmoor Cl. PL3: Ply . . . 1F **19**
Brynmoor Pk. PL3: Ply . . . 1F **19**
Brynmoor Wlk. PL3: Ply . . . 2F **19**
Buckfast Cl. PL2: Ply . . . 7J **11**
PL21: Ivy . . . 4E **24**
Buckingham Pl. PL5: Ply . . . 5G **11**
Buckland Cl. PL7: P'ton . . . 1E **20**
Buckland St.
PL1: Ply . . . 5C **4** (7B **18**)
Buckland Ter. PL20: Yel . . . 5C **38**
Buckwell St.
PL1: Ply . . . 5F **5** (7D **18**)
Buctor Pk. PL19: Tav . . . 4B **36**
Buddle Cl. PL9: P'ock . . . 4B **30**
PL19: Tav . . . 2D **36**
PL21: Ivy . . . 3F **25**
Budleigh Cl. PL9: P'ock . . . 4A **30**
Budshead Grn. PL5: Ply . . . 3B **12**
Budshead Rd. PL5: Ply . . . 4J **11**
PL6: Ply . . . 4D **12**
Budshead Way PL6: Ply . . . 5D **12**
Buena Vista Cl. PL6: Ply . . . 1J **13**
Buena Vista Dr. PL6: Ply . . . 1H **13**
Buena Vista Gdns. PL6: Ply . . . 1H **13**
Buena Vista Way PL6: Ply . . . 1H **13**
Bulleid Cl. PL2: Ply . . . 1J **17**
Buller Cl. PL7: P'ton . . . 4G **21**
PL11: Torp . . . 5D **16**
Buller Pk. PL12: Salt . . . 4A **10**
Buller Rd. PL11: Torp . . . 5E **16**
Bull Point Barracks
PL5: Ply . . . 7E **10**
Bulmer Rd. PL4: Ply . . . 4K **5** (6F **19**)
Bulteel Gdns. *PL6: Ply . . . 7D 6*
(off Winnicott Clo.)
Bunyan Cl. PL5: Ply . . . 5B **12**
Burleigh La. PL3: Ply . . . 1C **18**
Burleigh Mnr. PL3: Ply . . . 1C **18**
Burleigh Pk. Rd. PL3: Ply . . . 2C **18**
Burnard Cl. PL6: Ply . . . 7D **6**
Burnett Cl. PL12: Salt . . . 5A **10**
Burnett Rd. PL6: Ply . . . 7E **12**
Burnham Pk. Rd. PL3: Ply . . . 1C **18**
Burniston Cl. PL7: P'ton . . . 5H **21**
Burns Av. PL5: Ply . . . 5A **12**
BURRATON . . . 4A 10
BURRATON COOMBE . . . 5J 9
Burraton Rd. PL12: Salt . . . 3J **9**
Burrington Ind. Est.
PL5: Ply . . . 6K **11**
Burrington Rd. PL5: Ply . . . 6K **11**
Burrington Way PL5: Ply . . . 6K **11**
Burrow Hill PL9: P'ock . . . 3K **29**
Burton Cl. PL6: Ply . . . 1G **13**
Burwell Cl. PL6: Ply . . . 3K **13**
Bush Pk. PL6: Ply . . . 4A **14**
Butcher Pk. Hill PL19: Tav . . . 1D **36**
Bute Rd. PL4: Ply . . . 4F **19**
Butler Cl. PL6: Ply . . . 1G **13**
Butterdon Wlk. PL21: Ivy . . . 3G **25**
Butterdown PL12: Salt . . . 4J **9**
Butterpark PL21: Ivy . . . 3E **24**
Butt Pk. Rd. PL5: Ply . . . 5A **12**
Buttsford Ter. *PL21: L Mil . . . 4G 23*
(off The Avenue)
BUTTS PARK . . . 3J 35
Butts Pk. Ct. PL8: N Fer . . . 4J **35**
Byard Cl. PL5: Ply . . . 6H **11**
Byland Rd. PL3: Ply . . . 2F **19**
Byron Av. PL5: Ply . . . 5A **12**

C

Cabot Cl. PL12: Salt . . . 5B **10**
Cadleigh Cl. PL21: L Mil . . . 4K **23**
Cadleigh La. PL21: Ivy . . . 3A **24**
CADLEIGHPARK . . . 4K 23
Cadover Cl. PL6: Ply . . . 6F **13**
Caernarvon Gdns. PL2: Ply . . . 1A **18**
Calder Cl. PL3: Ply . . . 2G **19**
Caldicot Gdns. PL6: Ply . . . 6G **7**
Caledonia Cl. PL7: P'ton . . . 3J **21**
California Cotts. PL20: Hor . . . 1C **38**

Colebrook La.—Derriford

Colebrook La. PL7: P'ton 1F **21**
Colebrook Rd. PL5: Ply 6G **11**
PL7: P'ton 2F **21**
Cole La. PL21: Ivy 7C **24**
(Higher Keaton)
PL21: Ivy 2E **24**
(Ivybridge)
Coleman Dr. PL9: P'ock 4A **30**
Cole Moore Mdw.
PL19: Tav 2D **36**
Coleridge Av. PL6: Ply 5E **12**
Coleridge Gdns.
PL4: Ply 1K **5** (5F **19**)
Coleridge Rd.
PL4: Ply 1J **5** (4E **18**)
Colesdown Hill PL9: P'ock 1B **30**
Colin Campbell Ct.
PL1: Ply 4C **4** (6B **18**)
Collaford Cl. PL7: P'ton 5H **21**
College Av. PL4: Ply 3D **18**
PL19: Tav 2F **37**
College Dean Cl. PL6: Ply 2H **13**
College La. PL4: Ply 4D **18**
College Pk. Pl. PL3: Ply 3D **18**
College Rd. PL2: Ply 3H **17**
College Vw. PL3: Ply 4D **18**
Colliers Cl. PL9: Wem 3C **34**
Collin Cl. PL5: Ply 6G **11**
Collingwood Av. PL4: Ply 7F **19**
Collingwood Rd. PL1: Ply 5K **17**
Collingwood Vs. PL1: Ply 5K **17**
Colne Gdns. PL3: Ply 3G **19**
Colston Cl. PL6: Ply 1G **13**
Coltishall Cl. PL5: Ply 3J **11**
Coltness Rd. PL9: Elb 4C **30**
Coltsfield Cl. PL6: Ply 7G **13**
Colwill Rd. PL6: Ply 4K **13**
Colwill Wlk. PL6: Ply 4A **14**
Colwyn Rd. PL11: Torp 5D **16**
COMBE 4F **31**
Combe Down La.
PL8: N May 6G **35**
Combe La. PL8: Brix 4F **31**
Combley Dr. PL6: Ply 3J **13**
Commercial Ope PL4: Ply 6J **5**
Commercial Pl. PL4: Ply 7J **5**
Commercial Rd.
PL4: Ply 6J **5** (7E **18**)
PL20: Hor 2B **38**
Commercial St.
PL4: Ply 6J **5** (7E **18**)
Common La. PL6: Rob 1E **6**
Compass Dr. PL7: P'ton 1H **21**
Compton Av. PL3: Ply 3E **18**
Compton Knoll Cl. PL3: Ply . . .2F **19**
Compton Leigh PL3: Ply 2F **19**
Compton Pk. Rd. PL3: Ply 3E **18**
Compton Va. PL3: Ply 3F **19**
Congreve Gdns. PL5: Ply 6B **12**
Coniston Gdns. PL6: Ply 3E **12**
Connaught Av. PL4: Ply 4D **18**
Connaught La. PL4: Ply 4D **18**
Conqueror Dr. PL5: Ply 6D **12**
Conrad Rd. PL5: Ply 6B **12**
Consort Cl. PL3: Ply 1D **18**
Constable Cl. *PL5: Ply 5C 12*
(off Cowley Rd.)
Constance Pl.
PL1: Ply 3A **4** (6A **18**)
Constantine St.
PL4: Ply 4G **5** (6D **18**)
Convent Cl. PL12: Salt 4B **10**
Conway Gdns. PL2: Ply 1A **18**
Conyngham Ct. PL6: Ply 7F **13**
Cooban Ct. PL6: Ply 7F **13**
Cook Ct. PL12: Salt 4J **9**
Cookworthy Rd. PL2: Ply 2J **17**
Coombe End PL10: Kin 7D **26**
Coombe La. PL5: T Fol 1B **12**
Coombe Pk. PL10: Kin 7D **26**
PL12: Salt 5C **10**
Coombe Pk. Cl. PL10: Kin 7D **26**
Coombe Pk. La. PL5: Ply 4K **11**
Coombe Rd. PL12: Salt 6C **10**
Coombe Vw. *PL2: Ply 1H 17*
(off Ainslie Ter.)
Coombe Way PL5: Ply 6J **11**
Coplestone Rd. PL6: Ply 2C **12**
Coppard Mdws. PL7: P'ton 2C **20**
Copper Beech Way
PL6: Ply 7H **7**
Copperfields PL20: Hor 2A **38**
Coppers Pk. PL6: Ply 7K **7**
Coppice, The PL21: Ivy 4B **24**
Coppice Gdns. PL5: Ply 5D **12**
Coppice Wood Dr.
PL6: Ply 6H **7**
Copse Cl. PL7: P'ton 4E **20**
Copse Rd. PL7: P'ton 4E **20**
Copthorne Gdns.
PL9: P'ock 4A **30**
Corea Ter. PL1: Dev 6K **17**
Corfe Av. PL3: Ply 1E **18**
Corfe Cl. PL21: Ivy 4E **24**
Coringdean Cl. PL6: Ply 1G **13**
Corner Brake PL6: Ply 7J **7**
Cornfield Gdns. PL7: P'ton 1J **21**
Cornwall Beach PL1: Dev 6G **17**
Cornwall St. PL1: Dev 6G **17**
PL1: Ply 4C **4** (6B **18**)
(not continuous)
Cornwall St. Flats *PL1: Dev . . .6G 17*
(off Cornwall St.)
Cornwood Rd. PL7: P'ton 4J **21**
PL21: Ivy 3B **24**
Cornworthy Cl. PL2: Ply 1K **17**
Coronation Cotts.
PL11: Torp 5E **16**
Coronation Pl. PL5: Ply 7H **11**
Corondale Rd. PL2: Ply 1A **18**
Corporation Rd. PL2: Ply 1C **18**
Corsham Cl. PL6: Ply 1G **13**
Cory Ct. PL9: Wem 2D **34**
Cosdon Pl. PL6: Ply 6E **12**
Costly St. PL21: Ivy 3E **24**
Cotehele Av. PL2: Ply 3J **17**
PL4: Ply 5K **5** (7F **19**)
Cot Hill PL7: P'ton 3C **20**
Cot Hill Cl. PL7: P'ton 2B **20**
Cot Hill Dr. PL7: P'ton 3C **20**
Cot Hill Trad. Est.
PL7: P'ton 2B **20**
Cottage M. PL7: P'ton 4F **21**
Cotton Cl. PL7: P'ton 4G **21**
County Cl. PL7: P'ton 3H **21**
Court, The PL6: Ply 7H **7**
PL12: Salt 5K **9**
Courtenay Rd. PL19: Tav 2D **36**
Courtenay St.
PL1: Ply 5D **4** (6C **18**)
Courtfield Rd. PL3: Ply 3E **18**
Courtland Cres. PL7: P'ton 1E **20**
Courtlands PL12: Salt 6B **10**
Courtlands Cl. PL19: Tav 2D **36**
Courtlands Rd. PL19: Tav 2D **36**
Court Rd. PL8: N Fer 5E **34**
(not continuous)
Court Vw. PL8: Brix 5G **31**
Court Wood PL8: N Fer 4F **35**
Cove Mdw. PL11: Wil 2D **16**
Coverdale Pl. PL5: Ply 6A **12**
Cowdray Cl. PL12: Salt 5B **10**
Cowdray Ter. PL12: Salt 6B **10**
Cowley Rd. PL5: Ply 4C **12**
Cox's Cl. PL6: Ply 6G **13**
COXSIDE 6J **5** (1E **28**)
Cox Tor Cl. PL20: Yel 5C **38**
Cox Tor Rd. PL19: Tav 3G **37**
Coypool Rd. PL7: P'ton 2B **20**
CRABTREE 3J **19**
Crabtree Cl. PL3: Ply 3A **20**
Crabtree Vs. PL3: Ply 3K **19**
Crackston Cl. PL6: Ply 1G **19**
Craigie Dr. PL1: Ply 3A **4** (6A **18**)
Craigmore Av. PL2: Ply 3J **17**
Cramber Cl. PL6: Rob 5H **7**
PL19: Tav 4D **36**
Cranbourne Av.
PL4: Ply 2K **5** (5F **19**)
Cranfield PL7: P'ton 1D **20**
Cranmere Rd. PL3: Ply 2F **19**
Crantock Ter. PL2: Ply 3K **17**
Crapstone Rd. PL20: Yel 6B **38**
Crashaw Cl. PL5: Ply 4C **12**
Craven Av. PL4: Ply 2K **5** (5F **19**)
Crawford Rd.
PL1: Ply 1A **4** (5A **18**)
Creamery Cl. PL8: Torr 6D **32**
Crease La. PL19: Tav 3A **36**
Crediton Wlk. PL6: Ply 7K **13**
Creedy Rd. PL3: Ply 3H **19**
Crelake Cl. PL19: Tav 4E **36**
Crelake Ind. Est.
PL19: Tav 4D **36**
Crelake Pk. PL19: Tav 4E **36**
Crelake Vs. PL19: Tav 4E **36**
CREMYLL 2H **27**
Cremyll Rd. PL11: Torp 6E **16**
Cremyll St. PL1: Ply 7K **17**
Crescent, The
PL1: Ply 5C **4** (7B **18**)
PL8: Brix 4H **31**
PL12: Lan 1C **8**
Crescent Av.
PL1: Ply 6C **4** (7B **18**)
Crescent Av. M. PL1: Ply 6C **4**
Crescent Gdns. PL21: Ivy 2D **24**
Crescent Rd. PL21: Ivy 2D **24**
Cressbrook Cl. PL6: Ply 5A **14**
Cressbrook Dr. PL6: Ply 5A **14**
Cressbrook Wlk. PL6: Ply 5K **13**
Crestfield Ri. PL21: Ivy 3C **24**
Cresthill Rd. PL2: Ply 1A **18**
Crofters Ct. PL21: Filh 4G **25**
Croft Pk. *PL6: Ply 7H 7*
(off Copper Beech Way)
Cromartie Rd. *PL4: Ply 7G 19*
(off Cavendish Rd.)
Cromer Cl. PL6: Ply 7F **7**
Cromer Wlk. PL6: Ply 7F **7**
Cromwell Ga. PL6: Ply 7H **7**
Cromwell Rd.
PL4: Ply 5K **5** (7F **19**)
Crookeder Cl. PL9: P'ock 4B **30**
Cross Hill PL2: Dev 4H **17**
Cross Pk. PL8: Brix 4J **31**
Cross Pk. Av. PL6: Ply 6E **12**
Cross Pk. Rd. PL6: Ply 6E **12**
PL9: Wem 3B **34**
Cross Pk. Way PL6: Ply 6E **12**
Crossway PL7: P'ton 1D **20**
Crossway Av. PL4: Ply 5G **19**
Crossways PL9: Wem 3B **34**
Crowndale Av. PL3: Ply 2F **19**
Crowndale Rd. PL19: Tav 6C **36**
Crown Gdns. PL6: Ply 6F **13**
CROWNHILL 6F **13**
Crownhill Fort 4E 12
Crownhill Fort Rd.
PL6: Ply 4E **12**
Crownhill Rd. PL5: Ply 4J **11**
Crow Pk. PL3: Ply 3E **18**
Croydon Gdns. PL5: Ply 3H **11**
Crozier Rd. PL4: Ply 4E **18**
Crylla Valley Cotts.
PL12: Nott 1D **8**
Cuffe Rd. PL3: Ply 4A **18**
Culbin Grn. PL6: Ply 7J **13**
Culdrose Cl. PL5: Ply 4H **11**
Culme Rd. PL3: Ply 3F **19**
Culver Cl. PL6: Ply 7F **13**
Culver Ct. *PL12: Salt 5C 10*
(off Culver Rd.)
Culver Rd. PL12: Salt 5C **10**
Culver Way PL6: Ply 7E **12**
Culverwood Cl. PL7: P'ton 2K **21**
Cumberland Rd. PL1: Dev 7J **17**
Cumberland St. PL1: Dev 6H **17**
Cumble Tor La. PL12: Trem 4E **8**
Cundy Cl. PL7: P'ton 1B **20**
Cunliffe Av. PL9: Hoo 3F **29**
Cunningham Rd. PL5: T Fol 6B **6**
Cunningham Way
PL12: Salt 4A 10
(off Callington Rd.)
Curlew M. PL3: Ply 4H **19**
Cursons Way PL21: Ivy 3B **24**
Curtis St. PL1: Dev 7H **17**
Custom Ho. La.
PL1: Ply 7B **4** (1B **28**)
Cypress Cl. PL7: P'ton 3K **21**

D

Dairy La. PL1: Ply 2A **4** (5A **18**)
PL21: Ivy 3E **24**
Dale Av. PL6: Ply 1H **19**
Dale Gdns. PL4: Ply 4C **18**
Dale Rd. PL4: Ply 1D **4** (4C **18**)
Daleswood Rd. PL19: Tav 4C **36**
Dalton Gdns. PL5: Ply 4H **11**
Damerel Cl. PL1: Dev 6J **17**
Danum Dr. PL7: P'ton 5J **21**
Darklake Cl. PL6: Ply 2K **13**
Darklake La. PL6: Ply 6J **7**
Darklake Vw. PL6: Ply 2J **13**
Dark St. La. PL7: P'ton 3F **21**
Dart Cl. PL3: Ply 2J **19**
Dartington Wlk. PL6: Ply 7K **13**
Dartmeet Av. PL3: Ply 2G **19**
Dartmoor Country Holidays
PL20: Hor 1A **38**
Dartmoor National Pk.
Bittaford 1G 25
Roborough 1J 7
Tavistock 3J 37
Yelverton 4C 38
Dartmoor Vw. PL4: Ply 5H **19**
PL12: Salt 3B **10**
Dartmouth Wlk. PL6: Ply 7K **13**
(not continuous)
Darton Cotts. *PL12: Salt 4K 9*
(off Thorn La.)
Darwin Cres. PL3: Ply 3J **19**
Daucus Cl. PL19: Tav 4D **36**
Davenham Cl. PL6: Ply 1G **13**
David Cl. PL7: P'ton 2G **21**
Davids La. PL21: Filh 3H **25**
David Southgate Ct. PL1: Ply . . .5A **4**
Davy Cl. PL11: Torp 5C **16**
Davy Rd. PL6: Ply 3H **13**
Dawes La. PL9: Elb 2E **30**
PL10: Mill 4B **26**
Dawlish Wlk. PL6: Ply 1K **19**
Daws Ct. PL12: Salt 5D **10**
Dawson Cl. PL5: Ply 6H **11**
Daymond Rd. PL5: Ply 5G **11**
Dayton Cl. PL6: Ply 5D **12**
Deacon Cl. PL12: Salt 6C **10**
Deacon Dr. PL12: Salt 6C **10**
Deacons Grn. PL19: Tav 4C **36**
Dean Cross PL9: P'ock 2K **29**
Dean Cross Rd. PL9: P'ock . . .2K **29**
Dean Hill PL9: P'ock 2K **29**
Dean Pk. Rd. PL9: P'ock 2J **29**
Dean Rd. PL7: P'ton 1E **20**
Debden Cl. PL5: Ply 3G **11**
Deeble Cl. PL7: P'ton 1F **21**
Deep La. PL7: P'ton 6K **21**
Deer Leap PL19: Tav 4F **37**
Deer Pk. PL12: Salt 4C **10**
PL21: Ivy 3F **25**
Deer Pk. Cl. PL19: Tav 3E **36**
Deer Pk. Cres. PL19: Tav 3E **36**
Deer Pk. Dr. PL3: Ply 1H **19**
Deer Pk. La. PL19: Tav 3E **36**
Deer Pk. Rd. PL19: Tav 3E **36**
Defoe Cl. PL5: Ply 5B **12**
Delacombe Cl. PL7: P'ton 1G **21**
De-la-Hay Av.
PL3: Ply 1A **4** (5A **18**)
De-la-Hay Vs.
PL3: Ply 1A **4** (5A **18**)
Delamere Rd. PL6: Ply 1H **19**
Delamore Cl. PL21: Ivy 3B **24**
Delaware Gdns. PL2: Ply 1J **17**
Delgany PL6: Ply 2F **13**
Delgany Vw. PL6: Ply 2F **13**
Delgany Vs. PL6: Ply 2F **13**
Dell, The PL7: P'ton 2C **20**
PL19: Tav 2D **36**
Dengie Cl. PL7: P'ton 3J **21**
Denham Cl. PL5: Ply 5B **12**
Dennis Cl. PL5: Ply 1F **17**
Deptford Pl.
PL4: Ply 2G **5** (5D **18**)
Derby Rd. PL5: Ply 3B **12**
DERRIFORD 3G **13**

Derriford Bus. Pk. PL6: Ply 4F 13
Derriford Health & Leisure Cen.
........................3G 13
DERRIFORD HOSPITAL ...3G 13
Derriford Pk. PL6: Ply 4F 13
Derriford Rd. PL6: Ply 3F 13
Derry Av. PL4: Ply 1E 4 (5C 18)
Derry's Cross
PL1: Ply 5C 4 (7B 18)
Derwent Av. PL3: Ply 3H 19
Desborough La.
PL4: Ply 4K 5 (6F 19)
Desborough Rd.
PL4: Ply 4J 5 (6E 18)
Deveron Cl. PL7: P'ton 3H 21
Devonia Cl. PL7: P'ton 1F 21
DEVONPORT 5J 17
Devonport Column 7H 17
Devonport Hill PL1: Dev ..7J 17
PL10: Kin 7E 26
Devonport Rd. PL1: Dev ..6J 17
Devonport Rd. PL1: Dev ..6J 17
Devonport Station (Rail) ..5J 17
Devonshire Ct. PL11: Torp .5E 16
Devonshire Ho. PL1: Ply ..5B 4
Devonshire St. PL4: Ply ..3G 5
Devon Ter. PL3: Ply 4D 18
Devon Tors PL20: Yel 6D 38
Devon Tors Rd. PL20: Yel .5C 38
Dewar Wlk. PL5: Ply 5J 11
Diamond Av.
PL4: Ply 2H 5 (5E 18)
Dickens Rd. PL5: Ply 5A 12
Dickiemoor La. PL5: Ply ..5B 12
Dieppe Cl. PL1: Dev 5J 17
(off St Nazaire App.)
Digby Gro. PL6: Ply 2J 11
Dillons PL8: N Fer 5H 35
Dingle Rd. PL2: Ply 2K 17
PL7: P'ton 2D 20
Dingwall Av. PL5: Ply 4D 12
Dirty La. PL12: Car 2H 9
Discovery Quay PL1: Ply ..3E 4
Distine Cl. PL3: Ply 1G 19
Dittisham Wlk. PL6: Ply ..7K 13
Ditton Ct. PL6: Ply 7F 13
Dixon Pl. PL2: Dev 4J 17
Dixon Ter. PL8: Torr 6C 32
Dockray Cl. PL6: Ply 3J 13
Dockyard Station (Rail) ...4H 17
Doctors Steps PL8: N Fer ..6F 35
(off Yealm Rd.)
Dodbrook PL10: Mill 5B 26
Doddridge Cl. PL9: P'ock ..5A 30
Doidges Farm Cl. PL6: Ply .7G 13
Dolphin Bldg.
PL4: Ply 7H 5 (1E 28)
Dolphin Cl. PL9: P'ock ...3A 30
Dolphin Ct. Rd. PL9: P'ock .3A 30
Dolphin Av. PL4: Ply 5G 5
Dolphin Ho. PL4: Ply 5G 5
Dolphin Sq. PL9: P'ock ...2A 30
Dolvin Rd. PL19: Tav 3E 36
Donkey La. PL21: Ivy 3D 24
Donnington Dr. PL3: Ply ..1G 19
Dorchester Av. PL5: Ply ..3C 12
Doreena Rd. PL9: Elb 2D 30
Dormy Av. PL3: Ply 3E 18
Dorsmouth Ter. PL7: P'ton .4F 21
Douglas Dr. PL9: P'ock ...3B 30
Douglass Rd. PL3: Ply 2H 19
Douro Ct. PL21: Ivy 3E 24
Dousland Rd.
PL20: Dous, Yel 6D 38
Dovedale Rd. PL2: Ply 1K 17
Dove Gdns. PL3: Ply 2J 19
Dover Rd. PL6: Ply 4K 13
Down Cl. PL12: Salt 6K 9
Downfield Dr. PL7: P'ton ..3G 21
Downfield Wlk. PL7: P'ton .3G 21
Downfield Way PL7: P'ton .3G 21
Downgate Gdns. PL2: Ply ..7C 12
Downham Gdns. PL5: T Fol .7B 6
Downhorne Pk. PL9: P'ock .3A 30
Downlea PL19: Tav 4F 37
Down Pk. Dr. PL19: Tav ...4F 37
Down Rd. PL7: P'ton 3K 21
PL19: Tav 4E 36

Downside Av. PL6: Ply 1H 19
DOWN THOMAS 7H 29
Downton Cl. PL1: Ply ..2A 4 (5A 18)
Drake Cir. PL4: Ply ...3F 5 (6D 18)
Drake Ct. PL4: Ply 6E 18
PL5: Ply 3H 11
Drakefield Dr. PL12: Salt ..4D 10
Drake Gdns. PL19: Tav 4E 36
Drake Odeon Cinema 5D 4
(off Anthenaeum Pl.)
Drake Rd. PL19: Tav 2D 36
Drakes Cl. PL6: Ply 2E 12
Drake Statue 7D 4 (1C 28)
Drake Vs. PL19: Tav 4D 36
Drake Way PL9: P'ock 2K 29
Drax Gdns. PL6: Ply 7D 12
Drayton Rd. PL5: Ply 6B 12
Drive, The PL3: Ply 1D 18
Drovers Way PL21: Ivy 2B 24
Drummond Cl. PL2: Ply ...1J 17
Drummond Pl. PL1: Dev ...5J 17
Drunken Bri. Hill
PL7: P'ton 5D 20
Dryburgh Cres. PL2: Ply ..1K 17
Dryden Av. PL5: Ply 6B 12
Ducane Wlk. PL6: Ply 6G 13
Duck La. PL12: Trem 3F 9
Duckworth St. PL2: Dev ..4K 17
Ducky La. PL12: Lan 1C 8
Dudley Gdns. PL6: Ply 7G 13
Dudley Rd. PL7: P'ton 3C 20
Dukes Ryde, The
PL9: P'ock 2A 30
Duke St. PL1: Dev 6H 17
PL19: Tav 3E 36
Duloe Gdns. PL2: Ply 7B 12
Dumfries Av. PL5: Ply 4C 12
Duncan St. PL1: Dev 7H 17
Dunclair Pk. PL3: Ply 3J 19
Dundas St. PL2: Dev 4K 17
Dundonald St. PL2: Dev ..4J 17
Dunheved Rd. PL12: Salt ..5C 10
Dunkeswell Cl. PL2: Ply ..7J 11
Dunley Wlk. PL6: Ply 6H 13
Dunnet Rd. PL6: Ply 1C 12
Dunstan Dr. PL6: Ply 2E 12
Dunster Cl. PL7: P'ton 4K 21
Dunsterville Rd. PL21: Ivy .2F 25
DUNSTONE 5F 33
Dunstone Av. PL9: P'ock ..2B 30
Dunstone Cl. PL9: P'ock ..2A 30
Dunstone Cotts. PL8: Duns .5F 33
Dunstone Dr. PL9: P'ock ..2A 30
Dunstone La. PL9: Elb 2C 30
Dunstone Rd. PL5: Ply 4J 11
PL9: P'ock 2A 30
Dunstone Vw. PL9: P'ock ..2B 30
Durban Rd. PL3: Ply 3C 18
Durham Av. PL4: Ply ..2K 5 (5F 19)
Durham Cotts. PL1: Ply ...3B 4
Durnford St. PL1: Dev 7K 17
Durnford St. Ope PL1: Ply .7K 17
Durrant Cl. PL1: Dev 5H 17
Durris Cl. PL6: Ply 3J 13
Durris Gdns. PL6: Ply 3J 13
Durwent Cl. PL9: Hoo 3F 29
Duxford Cl. PL5: Ply 2H 11
Dymond Ct. PL12: Salt 5C 10
Dynevor Cl. PL3: Ply 1E 18

E

Eagle Rd. PL7: P'ton 3K 21
Earl's Acre PL3: Ply ...1B 4 (4B 18)
Earls Dr. PL10: Kin, Mill ..7D 26
Earls Mill Rd. PL7: P'ton ..2F 21
Earls Wood Cl. PL6: Ply ..4A 14
Earls Wood Dr. PL6: Ply ..4A 14
Eastbury Av. PL5: Ply 5K 11
East End PL9: P'ock 1H 29
Eastella Rd. PL20: Yel 6D 38
Easterdown Cl. PL9: P'ock .2A 30
Eastern Wood Rd.
PL7: P'ton 3A 22

Eastfield Av. PL9: Hoo 3H 29
Eastfield Cres. PL3: Ply ...1F 19
Eastlake St. PL1: Ply ...3E 4 (6C 18)
East Pk. Av. PL4: Ply ..1E 4 (5C 18)
East St. PL1: Ply 5A 4 (7A 18)
(not continuous)
East Vw. PL3: Ply 4K 17
(off Park St. Ope)
East Way PL21: L Mil 4J 23
Ebrington St.
PL4: Ply 4G 5 (6D 18)
Eddystone Cl. PL3: Ply ...2H 19
Eddystone Ter. PL1: Ply ..1B 28
Eddy Thomas Wlk. PL5: Ply .3B 12
Eden Cotts. PL21: Ivy 3E 24
Edgar Ter. PL4: Ply 4F 19
Edgcumbe Av. PL1: Ply ...7K 17
Edgcumbe Cres. PL10: Mill .3C 26
Edgcumbe Pk. Rd. PL3: Ply .2C 18
Edgcumbe St. PL1: Ply ...7K 17
Edgcumbe Dr. PL19: Tav ..2D 36
Edgecumbe Ho. PL1: Ply ..5A 4
Edgecumbe Rd. PL12: Salt .2K 9
Edinburgh St. PL1: Dev ...7H 17
Edith Av. PL4: Ply 5F 19
Edith St. PL5: Ply 6G 11
Edna Ter. PL4: Ply 6G 19
Edwards Cl. PL7: P'ton ...4J 21
Edwards Cres. PL12: Salt ..5K 9
Edwards Dr. PL7: P'ton ...3J 21
Effingham Cres. PL3: Ply ..1C 18
EFFORD 3H 19
Efford Crematorium
PL3: Ply 2H 19
Efford Cres. PL3: Ply 2G 19
Efford La. PL3: Ply 4G 19
Efford Pathway PL3: Ply ..2H 19
(not continuous)
Efford Rd. PL3: Ply 2G 19
Efford Wlk. PL3: Ply 2G 19
Egerton Cres.
PL4: Ply 3K 5 (6F 19)
Egerton Pl. PL4: Ply ..3K 5 (6F 19)
Egerton Rd. PL4: Ply ..4J 5 (6E 18)
EGGBUCKLAND 7G 13
Eggbuckland Rd. PL3: Ply ..2E 18
PL6: Ply 7G 13
Egret Cl. PL10: Mill 3D 26
Eight Acres Cl. PL7: P'ton .3K 21
Elaine Cl. PL7: P'ton 3C 20
Elbow La. PL19: Tav 2E 36
Elbridge Cotts. PL8: Brix ..4H 31
ELBURTON 2D 30
Elburton Rd.
PL9: Elb, P'ock 1B 30
Eldad Hill PL1: Ply 3A 4 (6A 18)
Elder Cl. PL7: P'ton 3J 21
Elford Cres. PL7: P'ton ...1F 21
Elford Dr. PL9: P'ock 2H 29
Elford Pk. PL20: Yel 6D 38
Elgin Cres. PL5: Ply 4D 12
Elim Ter. PL3: Ply 3D 18
Eliot St. PL5: Ply 7H 11
Elizabethan House 6F 5
Elizabeth Cl. PL21: Ivy ...3G 25
Elizabeth Pl.
PL4: Ply 2F 5 (5D 18)
Elliot St. PL1: Ply 7C 4 (1B 28)
Elliott Cl. PL12: Salt 5A 10
Elliott Ter. PL1: Ply 7D 4
Elliott Ter. La.
PL1: Ply 7D 4 (1C 28)
Elliott Rd. PL4: Ply 7F 19
Elliotts Hill PL8: Brix 5H 31
Elm Cl. PL19: Tav 5E 36
Elm Cotts. PL12: Salt 4K 9
(off Thorn La.)
Elm Cres. PL3: Ply 4F 19
Elm Cft. PL6: Ply 1J 13
(off Elm Rd.)
Elmcroft PL5: Ply 1A 18
Elm Gro. PL6: Ply 7G 13
PL7: P'ton 3F 21
Elm Pk. PL10: Mill 2E 26
Elm Rd. PL4: Ply 3E 18
PL6: Ply 1J 13

Elms, The PL3: Ply 5K 17
Elm Ter. PL4: Ply 3E 18
(off Elm Rd.)
Elm Tree Cl. PL8: Yeal ...5C 32
Elm Tree Pk. PL8: Yeal ...5C 32
Elmwood Cl. PL6: Ply 2J 13
Elphinstone Rd. PL2: Ply ..1B 18
Elwell Rd. PL12: Salt 4D 10
Elwick Gdns. PL3: Ply 3G 19
Embankment La. PL4: Ply ..6G 19
Embankment Rd.
PL4: Ply 5K 5 (7F 19)
Embankment Rd. La. Nth.
PL4: Ply 6G 19
(off Cathcart Av.)
Emily Gdns. PL4: Ply ..1J 5 (5E 18)
Emma Pl. PL1: Ply 7K 17
Emma Pl. Ope PL1: Ply ...7K 17
Endsleigh Gdns.
PL4: Ply 2F 5 (5D 18)
Endsleigh Pk. Rd. PL3: Ply .2C 18
Endsleigh Pl.
PL4: Ply 2F 5 (5D 18)
Endsleigh Rd. PL9: P'ock ..2H 29
Endsleigh Vw. PL21: Ivy ..3B 24
Eningdale Rd. PL19: Tav ..4C 36
Ennerdale Gdns. PL6: Ply ..3D 12
Enterprise Cl. PL11: Torp ..6E 16
Epping Cres. PL6: Ply 1J 13
Epworth Ter. PL2: Ply 3J 17
Eric Rd. PL4: Ply 4K 5 (6F 19)
Erith Av. PL2: Ply 1J 17
Erle Gdns. PL7: P'ton 5G 21
Erlstoke Cl. PL6: Ply 6J 13
Erme Cl. PL21: Ivy 3E 24
Erme Dr. PL21: Ivy 3D 24
Erme Gdns. PL3: Ply 3H 19
Erme M. PL21: Ivy 4D 24
Erme Rd. PL21: Ivy 3E 24
Erme Ter. PL21: Ivy 3E 24
Ermington Rd. PL21: Ivy ..4C 24
Ermington Ter. PL4: Ply ..4D 18
ERNESETTLE 3H 11
Ernesettle Cres. PL5: Ply ..4H 11
Ernesettle Grn. PL5: Ply ..3H 11
Ernesettle La. PL5: Ply ...2G 11
Ernesettle Rd. PL5: Ply ...4H 11
Ernesettle Ter. PL5: Ply ...4H 11
(off Ernesettle Rd.)
Erril Retail Pk. PL7: P'ton .3C 20
Esmonde Gdns. PL5: Ply ..7E 10
Esplanade, The
PL1: Ply 7D 4 (1C 28)
ESSA 5C 10
Essa Rd. PL12: Salt 5C 10
Essex St. PL1: Ply 2B 4 (5B 18)
Esso Wharf Rd.
PL4: Ply 7K 5 (1F 29)
ESTOVER 4K 13
Estover Cl. PL6: Ply 3A 14
Estover Ind. Est. PL6: Ply ..3A 14
Estover Rd. PL6: Ply 3K 13
Estover Sports Cen. 5J 13
Eton Av. PL1: Ply 2D 4 (5C 18)
Eton Pl. PL1: Ply 2D 4 (5C 18)
Eton St. PL1: Ply 3D 4 (5C 18)
Eton Ter. PL1: Ply 3C 4 (6B 18)
Evans Pl. PL2: Ply 3A 18
Evelyn Pl. PL4: Ply ...1F 5 (5D 18)
Evelyn St. PL5: Ply 6G 11
Evenden Ct. PL11: Torp ..5D 16
Exchange St. PL4: Ply 6F 5
Exe Gdns. PL3: Ply 1H 19
Exeter Cl. PL5: Ply 3G 11
Exeter Rd. PL21: Filh, Ivy ..3E 24
Exeter St. PL4: Ply 5F 5 (6D 18)
Exmouth Rd. PL1: Dev ...5J 17
(not continuous)
Explorer Ct. PL2: Ply 3A 18

F

Fairfax Ter. PL2: Ply 4J 17
Fairfield PL7: P'ton 1F 21
Fairfield Av. PL2: Ply 1B 18
Fairmead M. PL12: Salt ...4K 9

Fairmead Rd. PL12: Salt 5K 9
Fairview Av. PL3: Ply 3J 19
Fairview Way PL3: Ply 3K 19
Fairway PL12: Salt 5K 9
Fairway, The PL8: N Fer 5G 35
Fairway Av. PL21: Ivy 3C 24
Fanshawe Way PL9: Hoo ...3H 29
Faraday Mill Bus. Pk.
  PL4: Ply 7G 19
Faraday Rd. PL4: Ply 7G 19
Faringdon Rd. PL4: Ply 5G 19
Farm Cl. PL7: P'ton 2D 20
Farm La. PL5: Ply 5A 12
  PL12: Salt 6A 10
Farnley Cl. PL6: Ply 1G 13
Farriers Cotts. PL7: P'ton 2F 21
Fayre Vw. PL12: T'han 6H 9
Fearnside Way PL12: Salt ...4K 9
Federation Rd. PL3: Ply 4H 19
Fegen Rd. PL5: Ply 6E 10
Fellowes La. PL1: Ply 5A 18
Fellowes Pl. PL1: Ply 6K 17
Fenten Pk. PL12: Salt 4C 10
Fernbank Av. PL21: Ivy 2B 24
Fern Cl. PL7: P'ton 3J 21
Ferndale Av. PL2: Ply 1H 17
Ferndale Cl. PL6: Ply 6J 7
Ferndale Rd. PL2: Ply 1H 17
Fernhill Cl. PL21: Ivy 3C 24
Fernleigh Rd. PL3: Ply 3E 18
Fern Mdw. PL19: Tav 2F 37
Ferrers Rd. PL5: Ply 6H 11
Ferry La. PL11: Torp 2A 16
Ferry Rd. PL1: Dev 5G 17
Ferry St. PL11: Torp 5F 17
Feversham Cl. PL7: P'ton 2J 21
FILHAM 4G 25
Filham Ind. Est. PL21: Ivy ...4E 24
  (off Blair Rd.)
Filham Moor Cl. PL21: Ivy ...4F 25
Fillace La. PL20: Hor 2B 38
Fillace Pk. PL20: Hor 2B 38
Fillham Moor La. PL21: Ivy ..3E 24
Fincer Dr. PL21: Ivy 2B 24
Finch Cl. PL3: Ply 4J 19
Finches Cl. PL9: Elb 2D 30
Findon Gdns. PL6: Ply 3J 13
Finewell St. PL1: Ply ...5E 4 (7C 18)
Finnigan Rd. PL4: Ply 1G 29
Fircroft Rd. PL2: Ply 1A 18
First Av. PL1: Dev 6K 17
  PL9: P'ock 1A 30
Firtree Ri. PL21: Ivy 3E 24
Firtree Rd. PL6: Ply 1K 13
  (off Glenfield Way)
Fisgard Way PL11: Torp 5A 16
Fisher Rd. PL2: Ply 3K 17
Fish Quay PL4: Ply 6H 5
Fistral Cl. PL11: Torp 4C 16
Fitzford Cotts. PL19: Tav 4C 36
Fitzroy Cl. PL1: Ply 5K 17
Fitzroy Ter. PL1: Ply 5K 17
Flamborough Rd. PL6: Ply ...7F 7
Flamborough Way
  PL6: Ply 1F 13
Flamsteed Cres. PL5: Ply 6H 11
Fleet St. PL2: Ply 2H 17
Fletcher Cres. PL9: P'ock 3B 30
Fletcher Way PL9: P'ock 3B 30
Fletemoor Rd. PL5: Ply 6G 11
Flete Vw. Ter. PL21: Bit 6K 25
Flora Cotts.
  PL1: Ply 5B 4 (7B 18)
Flora Ct. PL1: Ply 4B 4 (6B 18)
  (not continuous)
Flora St. PL1: Ply 5B 4 (7B 18)
Florence Pl. PL4: Ply 6F 19
Florence St. PL5: Ply 6G 11
Florida Gdns. PL3: Ply 2H 19
Floyd Cl. PL2: Ply 1J 17
Foliot Av. PL2: Ply 2K 17
Foliot Rd. PL2: Ply 1J 17
FORD
  PL2 ....3K 17
  PL8 ....7K 33
Ford Cl. PL21: Ivy 3B 24
FORDER 6K 9

Forder Hgts. PL6: Ply 6G 13
Forder Hill PL10: Kin 7C 26
Forder Valley Nature Reserve
  ....7J 13
Forder Valley Rd. PL6: Ply ...6G 13
Ford Hill PL2: Ply 3K 17
FORD PARK 3C 18
Ford Pk. PL4: Ply 4D 18
Ford Pk. La. PL4: Ply 4D 18
Ford Pk. Rd. PL4: Ply 4C 18
Ford Rd. PL8: Torr 5C 32
  PL9: Wem 3A 34
Ford St. PL19: Tav 3D 36
Forest Av. PL2: Ply 1B 18
Foresters Rd. PL9: P'ock 2J 29
Fore St. PL1: Dev 6H 17
  PL5: T Fol 1A 12
  PL7: P'ton 4F 21
  PL8: Yeal 5C 32
  PL10: Kin 7D 26
  PL10: Mill 4B 26
  PL11: Torp 5E 16
  PL12: Salt 5C 10
  PL21: Ivy 3D 24
Forest Vw. PL6: Ply 7J 7
Forge Cl. PL6: Rob 5H 7
Forge La. PL12: Salt 3K 9
Forresters Dr. PL6: Ply 7J 7
Forsythia Dr. PL12: Salt 4J 9
Fort Austin Av. PL6: Ply 5E 12
Fortescue Pl. PL3: Ply 2F 19
Fortescue Ter. PL19: Tav 2C 36
Forth Gdns. PL3: Ply 2J 19
Fort Stamford Country Club ..3F 29
Fort Stamford the Ramparts
  PL9: Hoo 3F 29
Fort Ter. PL6: Ply 4E 12
Fosbrooke Ct. PL3: Ply 2E 18
Foulston Av. PL5: Ply 7E 10
Foundary La. PL8: N May 7G 35
Foundry La. PL8: N May 7G 35
Fountains Cres. PL3: Ply 7A 12
Fowey Gdns. PL3: Ply 2J 19
Fox Fld. Cl. PL3: Ply 3H 19
Foxglove Way PL12: Salt 4J 9
Foxtor Cl. PL5: Ply 4A 12
Foxwood Gdns. PL6: Ply 2D 12
Foyle Cl. PL7: P'ton 3H 21
Francis St. PL1: Ply 4A 4 (6A 18)
Frankfort Ga.
  PL1: Ply 4C 4 (6B 18)
Franklyns PL6: Ply 3F 13
Franklyns Cl. PL6: Ply 3F 13
Fraser Pl. PL5: T Fol 7B 6
Fraser Rd. PL5: T Fol 7B 6
Fraser Sq. PL5: T Fol 6B 6
Frederick St. E.
  PL1: Ply 4B 4 (6B 18)
Frederick St. W.
  PL1: Ply 4B 4 (6B 18)
Fredington Gro. PL2: Ply 2A 18
Freedom Sq. PL4: Ply 1H 5
Freeman's Wharf PL1: Ply ...1K 27
Freemantle Gdns. PL2: Ply ...4J 17
Freemantle Pl. PL2: Ply 4J 17
Frenchman's La. PL12: Nott ..1C 8
Frensham Av. PL6: Ply 1H 13
Frensham Gdns. PL6: Ply 7H 7
Freshford Cl. PL6: Ply 6H 13
Freshford Wlk. PL6: Ply 6H 13
Frewin Gdns. PL6: Ply 1G 13
Friars La. PL1: Ply 6F 5
Friars Wlk. PL19: Whit 6G 37
Friary Pk. PL4: Ply 4J 5 (6E 18)
Friary St. PL4: Ply 5H 5 (7E 18)
Frith Rd. PL12: Salt 4A 10
Frobisher App. PL5: Ply 5C 12
Frobisher Dr. PL12: Salt 5B 10
Frobisher Way PL11: Torp 5A 16
Frogmore Av. PL6: Ply 7G 13
Frogmore Ct. PL6: Ply 1G 19
Frome Cl. PL7: P'ton 4H 21
Frontfield Cres. PL6: Ply 2D 12
Fullerton Rd. PL2: Ply 3K 17

Furland Cl. PL9: Hoo 4H 29
Furneaux Av. PL2: Ply 3A 18
Furneaux Rd. PL2: Ply 3A 18
Fursdon Cl. PL9: Elb 3D 30
Furse Pk. PL5: Ply 1F 17
Furzeacre Cl. PL7: P'ton 1H 21
Furzehatt Av. PL9: P'ock 3B 30
Furzehatt Pk. Rd.
  PL9: P'ock 3B 30
Furzehatt Ri. PL9: P'ock 3B 30
Furzehatt Rd. PL9: P'ock 3A 30
Furzehatt Vs. PL9: P'ock 3A 30
Furzehatt Way PL9: P'ock 3B 30
Furzehill Rd.
  PL4: Ply 1H 5 (4E 18)

G

Gables, The PL7: P'ton 5D 20
GABLES, THE 5D 20
Galileo Cl. PL7: P'ton 2F 21
Gallacher Way PL12: Salt 4J 9
Gallops, The PL12: Salt 3A 10
Galsworthy Cl. PL5: Ply 5B 12
Galva Rd. PL7: Hem 7K 15
Ganges Rd. PL2: Ply 3K 17
Ganna Pk. Rd. PL3: Ply 2C 18
Gara Cl. PL9: Elb 3C 30
Garden Cl. PL7: P'ton 3A 22
Garden Cres.
  PL1: Ply 7B 4 (1B 28)
Garden La. PL19: Tav 3D 36
Garden Pk. Cl. PL9: Elb 2C 30
Garden St. PL2: Dev 4H 17
Garden Village PL9: P'ock 1A 30
Gards La. PL5: Ply 5H 11
Garfield Ter. PL1: Ply 5J 17
Garrett St. PL10: Kin 7D 26
Garrick Cl. PL5: Ply 5B 12
Garrison Cl. PL1: Dev 7H 17
Garrison Grn. PL1: Ply 6F 5
Garston Cl. PL9: P'ock 1B 30
Gascoyne Ct. PL4: Ply 4G 5
Gascoyne Pl.
  PL4: Ply 4G 5 (6D 18)
Gashouse La.
  PL4: Ply 6J 5 (7E 18)
Gasking St. PL4: Ply ...4G 5 (6D 18)
Gdynia Way PL4: Ply 5K 5 (7F 18)
Geasons La. PL7: P'ton 3F 21
Geffery Cl. PL12: Lan 1B 8
George Av. PL7: P'ton 2F 21
George La. PL7: P'ton 3G 21
  (not continuous)
George Pl. PL1: Ply 5A 4 (7A 18)
George Sq. PL1: Dev 7J 17
  (off Theatre Ope)
  PL1: Ply 7K 17
  (off Brownlow St.)
George St. PL1: Dev 7J 17
George St. La. E. PL1: Dev ...7J 17
Georgia Cres. PL3: Ply 2H 19
Gibbon La. PL4: Ply 3F 5 (6D 18)
Gibbon St. PL4: Ply 3F 5 (6D 18)
Gifford Pl. PL3: Ply 4C 18
Gifford Ter. Rd. PL3: Ply 3C 18
Gilbert Cl. PL7: P'ton 2J 21
Gilbert La. PL2: Ply 3B 18
Gilford Way PL21: L Mil 3K 23
Gill Pk. PL3: Ply 3G 19
Gilston Rd. PL12: Salt 3K 9
Gilwell Av. PL9: P'ock 2B 30
Gilwell Hall PL4: Ply 3F 5
Gilwell Pl. PL4: Ply 3F 5 (6D 18)
Gilwell St. PL4: Ply 3G 5 (6D 18)
Gin Distillery 6F 5
Gipsy La. PL21: Ivy 3A 24
Glade Cl. PL6: Ply 3F 13
Glanville Rd. PL19: Tav 3D 36
Glanvilles Mill PL21: Ivy 3D 24
Glanvilles Rd. PL21: Ivy 3E 24
Glanville St.
  PL4: Ply 3E 4 (6C 18)
Glanville Ter. PL12: Salt 3C 10
Glebe Av. PL12: Salt 4C 10
Glenavon Rd. PL3: Ply 3D 18

GLENBOURNE UNIT 4G 13
Glenburn Cl. PL3: Ply 1D 18
Glendower Rd. PL3: Ply 3C 18
Gleneagle Av. PL3: Ply 2E 18
Gleneagle Rd. PL3: Ply 2E 18
Gleneagle Vs. PL3: Ply 2E 18
  (off Gleneagle Av.)
Glenfield Cl. PL6: Ply 1J 13
Glenfield Rd. PL6: Ply 2H 13
Glenfield Way PL6: Ply 1J 13
Glenhaven Cl. PL7: P'ton 2K 21
GLENHOLT 1J 13
Glenholt Cl. PL6: Ply 1J 13
Glenholt Pk. PL6: Ply 1J 13
Glenholt Rd. PL6: Ply 1H 13
Glenhurst Rd. PL3: Ply 2D 18
Glenmore Av. PL2: Ply 3J 17
Glen Pk. Av.
  PL4: Ply 1E 4 (5C 18)
Glen Rd. PL3: Ply 3E 18
  PL7: P'ton 2E 20
Glenside Ri. PL7: P'ton 2F 21
Glentor Rd. PL3: Ply 1D 18
Glenwood Rd. PL3: Ply 2D 18
Globe Theatre 7K 17
Gloucester Ct. PL1: Ply 2D 4
Gloucester Pl.
  PL1: Ply 2D 4 (5C 18)
Goad Av. PL4: Ply 7F 19
Goad Cl. PL11: Torp 5C 16
Godding Gdns. PL6: Ply 7D 6
Godwell La. PL21: Ivy 5E 24
Golden Sq. PL7: P'ton 2F 21
Goldfinch Gro. PL12: Salt ...3A 10
Goldsmith Gdns. PL5: Ply 4C 12
Golf Links Rd. PL20: Yel 7C 38
Goodeve Cl. PL9: P'ock 3K 29
Goodwin Av. PL6: Ply 1F 13
Goodwin Cres. PL2: Ply 2K 17
Gooseberry La.
  PL1: Ply 6C 4 (7B 18)
GOOSEWELL 4A 30
Goosewell Hill PL6: Ply 7G 13
Goosewell Pk. Rd.
  PL9: P'ock 3A 30
Goosewell Rd. PL9: P'ock 3A 30
Goosewell Ter. PL9: P'ock ...3A 30
Gordon Ct. PL12: Salt 5A 10
Gordon Ter. PL4: Ply ...1F 5 (4D 18)
  PL10: Mill 4C 26
Gorse Way PL21: Ivy 4E 24
Gorsey Cl. PL5: Ply 5D 12
Goswela Cl. PL9: P'ock 4A 30
Goswela Gdns. PL9: P'ock ...4A 30
Gower Ridge Rd.
  PL9: P'ock 3J 29
Grafton Rd. PL4: Ply 4D 18
Grainge Rd. PL6: Ply 6F 13
Granby Cl. PL1: Dev 6H 17
Granby Grn. PL1: Dev 6H 17
Granby Pl. PL1: Dev 6H 17
Granby St. PL1: Dev 6H 17
Granby Way PL1: Dev 6H 17
Grand Hotel Rd.
  PL1: Ply 7C 4 (1B 28)
Grand Pde. PL1: Ply ...7C 4 (1B 28)
Grange Rd. PL7: P'ton 4G 21
  PL20: Yel 5C 38
Grantham Cl. PL7: P'ton 4C 20
Grantley Gdns. PL3: Ply 4F 19
Grasmere Cl. PL6: Ply 2D 12
Grassendale Av. PL2: Ply 1J 17
Grass La. PL2: Ply 2B 18
Grassmere Way PL12: Salt ...3A 10
Grassy La. PL8: Wors 3H 33
Gratton La. PL20: Yel 7D 38
Gratton Pl. PL6: Ply 6F 13
Gravesend PL11: Torp 5E 16
Gravesend Gdns.
  PL11: Torp 5E 16
Gravesend Wlk. PL5: Ply 3G 11
Graybridge Rd. PL20: Hor ...2B 38
Gray Cres. PL5: Ply 7F 11
Gt. Berry Rd. PL6: Ply 6D 12
Gt. Churchway PL9: P'ock ...2B 30
Greatfield Rd. PL3: Ply 1G 19

Hoe Ct.—Ladysmith Rd.

Hoe Ct. PL1: Ply 6D **4**
Hoe Gdns. PL1: Ply 6E **4**
Hoegate Pl. PL1: Ply 6E **4**
Hoegate St. PL1: Ply . . .6F **5** (7D **18**)
Hoe Rd. PL1: Ply 7C **4** (1B **28**)
Hoe St. PL1: Ply 6E **4** (7C **18**)
Hogarth Cl. PL9: Elb 3C **30**
Hogarth Ho. *PL19: Tav 2E **36***
(off Taylor Sq.)
Hogarth Wlk. PL9: Elb 3C **30**
HOLBETON **7K 33**
Holborn Pl. PL7: P'ton 2F **21**
Holborn St. PL4: Ply . . .5J **5** (7E **18**)
Holcombe Dr. PL9: P'ock 4A **30**
Holcroft Cl. PL12: Salt 5A **10**
Holdsworth St.
PL4: Ply 1C **4** (5B **18**)
Holebay Cl. PL9: P'ock 4B **30**
Hollacombe Brake
PL9: Wem 1C **34**
HOLLACOMBE HILL **7B 30**
Hollacombe Woods Nature Reserve
. . . .**7D 30**
Holland Rd. PL3: Ply 2D **18**
PL7: P'ton 3K **21**
PL9: P'ock 3A **30**
Holloway Gdns. PL9: P'ock . . .4B **30**
Hollowgutter La.
PL11: Torp 6A **16**
Hollow Hayes *PL6: Ply 7G **13***
(off Eggbuckland Rd.)
Hollows, The PL9: Elb 1C **30**
Holly Ct. PL6: Ply 1K **19**
Hollycroft Rd. PL3: Ply 1F **19**
Holly Pk. Cl. PL5: Ply 2K **11**
Holly Pk. Dr. PL5: Ply 2K **11**
Hollywood Ter. PL1: Ply 3A **4**
Holman Ct. PL2: Ply 7B **12**
Holmans Bldgs. PL1: Dev 6G **17**
Holman Way PL21: Ivy 2B **24**
Holmbush Way PL8: Brix 5H **31**
Holmer Down PL6: Ply 7J **7**
Holmes Av. PL3: Ply 3G **19**
Holmwood Av. PL9: P'ock 4K **29**
Holne Chase PL6: Ply 7G **7**
Holtwood Dr. PL21: Ivy 3B **24**
Holtwood Rd. PL6: Ply 1J **13**
Holwell Cl. PL9: P'ock 4B **30**
Holyrood Pl.
PL1: Ply 7D **4** (1C **28**)
Home Farm Rd. PL9: P'ock . . .1K **29**
Home Park **3B 18**
Home Pk. PL2: Dev 4J **17**
PL12: Lan 1B **8**
Home Pk. Av. PL3: Ply 2D **18**
Home Pk. Rd. PL12: Salt 4D **10**
Homer Pk. PL9: Hoo 4H **29**
PL12: Salt 4A **10**
Homer Pk. La. Sth.
PL9: Hoo 4H **29**
Homer Ri. PL9: Elb 2C **30**
Home Sweet Home Ter.
PL4: Ply 6K **5** (7F **19**)
Honcray PL9: P'ock 1J **29**
Honeysuckle Cl. PL6: Ply 7K **7**
PL12: Salt 3A **10**
HONICKNOWLE **5B 12**
Honicknowle Grn.
PL5: Ply 4A **12**
Honicknowle La. PL2: Ply 6A **12**
PL5: Ply 6A **12**
Honiton Cl. PL5: Ply 4A **12**
Honiton Wlk. PL5: Ply 3A **12**
HOOE **4H 29**
Hooe Hill PL9: Hoo 4H **29**
Hooe Lake PL10: Mill 5E **26**
Hooe La. PL9: Stad 5H **29**
Hooe Rd. PL9: Hoo 3G **29**
Hooksbury Av. PL7: P'ton 5J **21**
Hooper Cl. PL12: Lan 2B **8**
Hooper St. PL11: Torp 5F **17**
Hopton Cl. PL6: Ply 7E **12**
Hornbrook Gdns. PL6: Ply 1C **12**
Hornby St. PL2: Ply 4J **17**
Hornchurch La. PL5: Ply 3H **11**
Hornchurch Rd. PL5: Ply 2H **11**
Horn Cross Rd. PL9: P'ock 2K **29**
Horn La. PL8: Brix 4H **31**
PL9: P'ock 2K **29**
Horn La. Flats PL9: P'ock 2A **30**
HORRABRIDGE **2B 38**
Horseshoe Dr. PL7: P'ton 3E **20**
Horsham La. PL5: Ply 5B **12**
PL5: T Fol 6A **6**
(not continuous)
Horswell Cl. PL7: P'ton 3J **21**
Hosford Cl. PL9: P'ock 5A **30**
Hospital Rd.
PL4: Ply 2H **5** (5E **18**)
Hotham Pl. PL1: Ply . . .2A **4** (5A **18**)
Houldsworth Rd.
PL9: P'ock 2H **29**
Houndiscombe Rd.
PL4: Ply 1F **5** (5D **18**)
Hounster Dr. PL10: Mill 5A **26**
Hounster Hill PL10: Mill 4A **26**
Housman Cl. PL5: Ply 4C **12**
Howard Cl. PL5: Ply 5J **11**
PL12: Salt 4A **10**
PL19: Tav 3C **36**
Howard Ct. PL1: Ply 7B **4**
Howard Rd. PL9: P'ock 1K **29**
Howards Way PL21: Ivy 2B **24**
Howeston La. PL6: Ply 3F **13**
How St. PL4: Ply 5F **5** (7D **18**)
Humber Cl. PL3: Ply 2J **19**
Hungerford Rd. PL2: Ply 2A **18**
Hunsdon Rd. PL21: Ivy 5A **24**
Hunter Cl. PL6: Ply 5E **12**
Hunters Cl. PL21: Ivy 3C **24**
Huntingdon Gdns. PL5: Ply . . .3C **12**
Huntley Pl. PL3: Ply 4H **19**
Huntley Vs. PL3: Ply 4H **19**
Hurdwick Rd. PL19: Tav 3C **36**
Hurrabrook Cl. PL6: Ply 5K **13**
Hurrabrook Gdns. PL6: Ply . . .5K **13**
Hurrell Cl. PL6: Ply 1C **12**
Hurrell Ct. PL3: Ply 3H **19**
Hursley Bus. Pk. PL6: Rob 5K **7**
Hurst Cl. PL9: P'ock 4A **30**
Hutchings Cl. PL6: Ply 1C **12**
Huxham Cl. PL6: Ply 7F **13**
Huxley Cl. PL7: P'ton 1G **21**
Hyde Pk. Rd. PL3: Ply 3D **18**

I

Ilbert St. PL1: Ply 2C **4** (5B **18**)
Ince Cl. PL11: Torp 4B **16**
Inchkeith Rd. PL6: Ply 1E **12**
Ingra Rd. PL3: Ply 2F **19**
Ingra Tor Cl. PL20: Yel 5C **38**
Ingra Wlk. PL6: Rob 6G **7**
Instow Wlk. PL5: Ply 4K **11**
Inswell Ct. PL19: Tav 2C **36**
INSWORKE **3C 26**
Insworke Cl. PL10: Mill 3D **26**
Insworke Cres. PL10: Mill 3C **26**
Insworke Pl. PL10: Mill 3D **26**
Inverdene PL3: Ply 3C **18**
Ipswich Cl. PL5: Ply 3B **12**
Ivanhoe Rd. PL5: Ply 5G **11**
IVYBRIDGE **3E 24**
Ivybridge Rd. PL21: Erm 7F **25**
Ivybridge Station (Rail) **2G 25**
Ivybridge Viaduct **2E 24**
Ivydale Rd. PL4: Ply 4E **18**
Ivydene Rd. PL21: Ivy 3C **24**

J

Jackmans Mdw.
PL10: Kin 7D **26**
Jackson Cl. PL5: Ply 7H **11**
Jackson Pl. PL2: Dev 4J **17**
Jackson Way PL12: Salt 4B **10**
Jago Av. PL11: Torp 5D **16**
James Cl. PL9: Elb 2C **30**
James Pl. PL4: Ply 2E **4** (5C **18**)
James Rd. PL19: Whit 6G **37**
James St. PL1: Dev 7H **17**
PL4: Ply 3E **4** (6C **18**)
Jasmine Gdns. PL6: Ply 1K **13**
PL7: P'ton 3J **21**
Jean Cres. PL3: Ply 2G **19**
Jedburgh Cres. PL2: Ply 7K **11**
Jefferson Wlk.
PL3: Ply 1C **4** (5B **18**)
Jeffery Cl. PL6: Ply 1C **12**
Jellicoe Rd. PL5: Ply 6D **12**
Jenkins Cl. PL9: P'ock 4B **30**
Jennycliff La. PL9: Hoo 4F **29**
Jennyscombe Cl.
PL9: P'ock 5A **30**
Jephson Rd. PL4: Ply 5G **19**
Jessops PL7: P'ton 1E **20**
Jinkin Av. PL4: Ply 1J **5** (5E **18**)
John Gaynor Homes
PL4: Ply 4G **5**
Johnston Ter. La. E.
PL2: Ply 2H **17**
Johnston Ter. Ope PL2: Ply . . .2H **17**
John St. PL1: Dev 5H **17**
Jordan La. PL20: Hor 2B **38**
Jubilee Cl. PL12: Salt 5A **10**
PL21: Ivy 2G **25**
Jubilee Cotts. *PL6: Ply 7G **13***
(off Doidges Farm Clo.)
PL12: Salt 6A **10**
Jubilee Pl. *PL3: Ply 4H **19***
(off Huntley Pl.)
Jubilee Rd. PL5: Ply 4J **11**
Jubilee Ter. PL4: Ply 6G **19**
PL21: Bit 2K **25**
Julian Pl. PL2: Ply 3J **17**
Julian Rd. PL21: Ivy 3C **24**
Julian St. PL4: Ply 6K **5** (7F **19**)
Julian Wlk. PL6: Ply 1K **13**
Jump Cl. PL6: Rob 5H **7**
Juniper Way PL7: P'ton 3J **21**

K

Kathleaven St. PL5: Ply 6G **11**
Kay Cl. PL7: P'ton 1G **21**
Keaton La. PL21: Erm, Ivy 5E **24**
Keaton Rd. PL21: Ivy 4D **24**
Keat St. PL2: Dev 4H **17**
Kedlestone Av. PL5: Ply 4K **11**
Keep, The PL12: Salt 5K **9**
Kelly Cl. PL5: Ply 1F **17**
Kelvin Av. PL4: Ply 1K **5** (5F **19**)
Kempe Cl. PL2: Ply 2J **17**
Kempton Ter. PL11: Torp 5E **16**
Kemyell Pl. PL2: Dev 4H **17**
Kendal Pl. PL5: Ply 3D **12**
Kenilworth Rd. PL2: Ply 1A **18**
Kenley Gdns. PL5: Ply 3J **11**
Kenmare Dr. PL7: P'ton 3H **21**
Kenn Cl. PL5: Ply 4A **12**
Kennel Hill PL7: P'ton 4E **20**
Kennel Hill Cl. PL7: P'ton 4D **20**
Kennel La. PL21: Ivy 3B **24**
Kennels, The PL21: Ivy 2C **24**
Kennet Cl. PL3: Ply 2G **19**
Kensington Pl. PL4: Ply 4E **18**
Kensington Rd.
PL4: Ply 1H **5** (4E **18**)
Kent Rd. PL2: Ply 3J **17**
Keppel Pl. PL2: Dev 4J **17**
Keppel St. PL2: Dev 4J **17**
Keppel Ter. *PL2: Dev 4J **17***
(off Keppel St.)
Kernow Cl. PL11: Torp 5B **16**
Ker St. PL1: Dev 7H **17**
Ker St. Ope PL1: Dev 6H **17**
Kestrel Pk. PL5: Ply 6K **11**
Kestrel Way PL6: Ply 6J **7**
Keswick Cres. PL6: Ply 5J **13**
Keyes Cl. PL1: Dev 6J **17**
KEYHAM **2H 17**
Keyham Rd. PL2: Dev 4H **17**
Keyham Station (Rail) **2H 17**
Keyham St. PL5: Ply 7H **11**
Khyber Cl. PL11: Torp 5D **16**
Kidwelly Cl. PL7: P'ton 4K **21**
Kiel Pl. PL3: Ply 3J **19**
Killigrew Av. PL12: Salt 6A **10**
Kiln Cl. PL5: Ply 7F **11**
Kilnpark Wlk. PL11: Torp 2A **16**
Kilworthy Hill PL19: Tav 2E **36**
Kilworthy Pk. PL19: Tav 2E **36**
Kilworthy Rd. PL19: Tav 2E **36**
Kimberley Cotts. *PL12: Salt 4K **9***
(off Thorn La.)
Kimberly Dr. PL6: Ply 6G **13**
King Edward Rd. PL12: Salt . . .5C **10**
Kingfisher Cl. PL6: Ply 1K **13**
Kingfisher Way PL9: P'ock 2H **29**
King Gdns. PL1: Ply 3C **4**
KINGSAND **7D 26**
Kings Cl. PL6: Ply 1K **13**
Kings Ct. PL1: Dev 5K **17**
PL1: Ply 4A **4**
Kingsland Gdn. Cl.
PL3: Ply 2D **18**
Kingsley Av. PL11: Torp 6E **16**
Kingsley Cl. PL21: L Mil 4K **23**
Kingsley Rd. PL4: Ply 4D **18**
Kingsmill Rd. PL12: Salt 2A **10**
Kings Rd. PL1: Dev 6J **17**
PL5: Ply 4J **11**
KING'S TAMERTON **6J 11**
King's Tamerton Rd.
PL5: Ply 5H **11**
Kingston Cl. PL7: P'ton 3H **21**
Kingston Dr. PL7: P'ton 2H **21**
King St. PL1: Ply 4A **4** (6A **18**)
PL10: Mill 4B **26**
PL11: Torp 5F **17**
PL19: Tav 2D **36**
Kingsway Gdns. PL6: Ply 4E **12**
Kingswear Cres. PL6: Ply 6G **13**
Kingswood Pk. Av. PL3: Ply . . .2C **18**
Kinnaird Cres. PL6: Ply 7D **6**
Kinross Av. PL4: Ply . . .1K **5** (4F **19**)
Kinsale Rd. PL5: Ply 4J **11**
Kinterbury Rd. PL5: Ply 7E **10**
Kinterbury St.
PL1: Ply 5F **5** (7D **18**)
Kinterbury Ter. PL5: Ply 7E **10**
Kinver Cl. PL6: Ply 3J **13**
Kipling Gdns. PL5: Ply 5C **12**
Kirkby Pl. PL4: Ply 2E **4** (5C **18**)
Kirkby Ter. PL4: Ply 2E **4**
Kirkdale Gdns. PL2: Ply 1A **18**
Kirkella Rd. PL20: Yel 6D **38**
Kirkland Cl. PL6: Ply 7H **7**
Kirkstall Cl. PL2: Ply 1J **17**
Kirkwall Rd. PL5: Ply 4D **12**
(not continuous)
Kirton Pl. PL3: Ply 3G **19**
Kit Hill Cres. PL5: Ply 7F **11**
Kitley Vw. PL8: Brix 4J **31**
Kitley Way PL5: Ply 6H **11**
Kitter Dr. PL9: P'ock 4A **30**
Knapps Cl. PL9: Elb 3D **30**
Kneele Gdns. PL3: Ply 7D **12**
KNIGHTON **2D 34**
Knighton Hill PL9: Wem 2D **34**
Knighton Hill Bus. Cen.
PL9: Wem 2D **34**
Knighton Rd.
PL4: Ply 4J **5** (6E **18**)
PL9: Wem 2C **34**
Knighton Ter. PL20: Hor 1B **38**
Knill Cross PL10: Mill 4B **26**
Knoll, The PL7: P'ton 2C **20**
Knowland Cl. PL1: Dev 6J **17**
Knowle Av. PL2: Ply 2H **17**
Knowle Wlk. PL2: Ply 2J **17**
Kynance Cl. PL11: Torp 4C **16**

L

Laburnham Gro. *PL6: Ply 2J **13***
(off Beech Ct.)
Laburnum PL19: Tav 2E **36**
Laburnum Dr. PL9: Wem 3B **34**
Lady Fern Rd. PL6: Rob 5H **7**
Ladysmith Ct.
PL4: Ply 1K **5** (5F **19**)
Ladysmith Rd.
PL4: Ply 1K **5** (5F **19**)

Ladywell Av.—Manadon Cl.

Ladywell Av. *PL4: Ply* *3G* ***5*** *(off Ladywell Pl.)*
Ladywell Pl. PL4: Ply 3G **5** (6E **18**)
LAIRA 4H 19
Laira Av. PL3: Ply 4J **19**
Laira Bri. PL4: Ply 7H **19**
Laira Bri. Rd. PL4: Ply 6G **19**
Laira Gdns. PL3: Ply 4H **19**
Laira Pk. Cres. PL4: Ply 4G **19**
Laira Pk. Pl. PL4: Ply 4G **19**
Laira Pk. Rd. PL4: Ply 4G **19**
Laira Pl. PL4: Ply 4K **5** (6F **19**)
Laira St. PL4: Ply 4K **5** (6F **19**)
Laity Wlk. PL6: Ply 1C **12**
Lake La. PL20: Dous 5E **38**
Lake M. PL10: Mill 4B **26**
Lake Rd. PL9: Hoo 3G **29**
Lakeside PL19: Tav 2D **36**
Lakeside Dr. PL5: Ply 2G **11**
Lake Vw. Cl. PL5: Ply 1A **12**
Lake Vw. Dri PL5: Ply 1K **11**
Lake Vw. Dr. PL5: Ply 2K **11**
Lalebrick Rd. PL9: Hoo 4F **29**
Lambert Rd. *PL5: T Fol* *1A* ***12*** *(off Station Rd.)*
Lambhay Hill PL1: Ply 6F **5** (7D **18**)
Lambhay St. PL1: Ply 7F **5** (1D **28**)
Lamerton Cl. PL5: Ply 4A **12**
Lamorna Pk. PL11: Torp 5B **16**
Lancaster Gdns. PL5: Ply 3C **12**
Lander Rd. PL12: Salt 4C **10**
LANDRAKE 2B 8
Landrake Cl. PL5: Ply 7F **11**
Landreath Gdns. PL2: Ply 7C **12**
Lands Pk. PL9: P'ock 2A **30**
Landulph Gdns. PL5: Ply 7F **11**
Lane, The PL7: P'ton 2E **20**
LANGAGE 3A 22
Langage Ind. Est. PL7: P'ton 3A **22**
Langage Pk. PL7: P'ton 4A **22**
Langage Science Pk. PL7: P'ton 3A **22**
Langdale Cl. PL6: Ply 6J **13**
Langdale Gdns. PL6: Ply 6J **13**
Langdon Ct. PL9: Elb 3C **30**
Langdon Down Way PL11: Torp 5B **16**
Langerwell Cl. PL12: Salt 4K **9**
Langerwell La. *PL12: Salt* *4J* ***9*** *(off Hallett Cl.)*
PL12: Salt 4K **9** (Fairmead M.)
Lang Gro. PL9: Elb 2C **30**
PL19: Tav 3F **37**
Langham Levels PL21: Ivy 2C **24**
Langham Pl. PL4: Ply 6F **19**
Langham Way PL21: Ivy 3C **24**
Langhill Rd. PL3: Ply 3C **18**
Langlands Mdw. PL21: Ivy 4G **25**
Langley Cl. PL6: Ply 7F **7**
Langley Cres. PL6: Ply 7E **6**
Langmead Cl. PL6: Ply 7H **13**
Langmead Rd. PL6: Ply 7H **13**
Langmore Cl. PL6: Ply 7F **13**
Langstone Rd. PL2: Ply 1B **18**
Langstone Ter. PL2: Ply 1B **18**
Langton Rd. PL20: Yel 5C **38**
Lanhydrock Rd. PL4: Ply 3J **5** (6E **18**)
Lansdowne Rd. PL6: Ply 5E **12**
Lanteglos Cl. PL21: Bit 7K **25**
Lapthorn Cl. PL9: P'ock 2H **29**
Larch Cl. PL12: Salt 4K **9**
Larch Dr. PL6: Ply 7K **7**
Larkhall Ri. PL3: Ply 3G **19**
Larkham Cl. PL7: P'ton 2D **20**
Larkham La. PL7: P'ton 2C **20**
Lark Hill PL2: Ply 2K **17**
LATCHBROOK 4J 9
Latham Cl. PL6: Ply 1F **19**
Latimer Cl. PL7: P'ton 3J **21**
Latimer Wlk. PL6: Ply 7D **6**
Launceston Cl. PL6: Ply 7G **7**
Laurel Cotts. *PL5: Ply* *6G* ***11*** *(off Trelawny Rd.)*
Laurel Ct. PL2: Ply 1K **17**
Laurel Dene PL2: Ply 1K **17**
Laurel Dr. PL6: Ply 2K **13**
Laurel Rd. PL2: Ply 1K **17**
Lavington Cl. PL7: P'ton 3J **21**
Lavinia Dr. PL7: P'ton 3D **20**
Lawn, The PL19: Tav 2E **36**
Lawn Cl. PL7: P'ton 3K **21**
Lawns, The PL5: Ply 6D **12**
PL11: Torp 4D **16**
Lawrence Rd. PL9: Hoo 2E **28**
Lawson Gro. PL9: P'ock 2H **29**
Law Wlk. PL6: Ply 1C **12**
Leander Way PL5: Ply 5C **12**
Leanway PL12: Salt 5B **10**
Leatfield Dr. PL6: Ply 2D **12**
Leatherby Cl. PL6: Ply 7D **6**
Leather Tor Cl. PL20: Yel 5C **38**
Leatside PL6: Rob 5H **7**
Leat Vw. PL12: Salt 4J **9**
Leat Wlk. PL3: Ply 2D **18**
PL6: Rob 5H **7**
PL12: Salt *3A* ***10*** *(off Grassmere Way)*
Leaves Yd. PL3: Ply 2G **19**
Ledgate La. PL7: P'ton, S'ell 1C **22**
LEE MILL 4G 23
LEE MILL HOSPITAL 3J 23
Lee Mill Ind. Est. PL21: L Mil 4J **23**
Legion La. PL8: Brix 4H **31**
Legis Wlk. PL6: Rob 6G **7**
Leg O Mutton Cnr. PL20: Yel 6C **38**
LEIGHAM 6K 13
Leigham Mnr. Rd. PL6: Ply 1A **20**
Leigham St. PL1: Ply 7C **4** (1B **28**)
Leigham Ter. La. PL1: Ply 6C **4**
Leigh Cl. PL21: Bit 6K **25**
Leigh Ct. PL6: Ply 7F **13**
Leigh La. PL6: Rob 4J **7**
Leighton Rd. PL3: Ply 7D **12**
Leland Gro. PL21: Ivy 4E **24**
Leonards Rd. PL21: Ivy 3E **24**
Lester Cl. PL3: Ply 2G **19**
Lewes Gdns. PL5: Ply 3B **12**
Leyford Cl. PL9: Wem 3C **34**
Leyford La. PL9: Stad 6A **30**
Leypark Dr. PL6: Ply 5J **13**
Leypark Wlk. PL6: Ply 4K **13**
Liddle Way PL7: P'ton 2J **21**
Lifton Rd. PL4: Ply 5J **5** (7F **19**) (not continuous)
Lilac Cl. PL9: Hoo 4H **29**
Limerick Pl. PL4: Ply 4K **5** (6F **19**)
Limes, The PL6: Ply 5E **12**
Limetree Rd. PL3: Ply 1C **18**
Lincoln Av. PL4: Ply 1K **5** (5F **19**)
Linden Ter. PL4: Ply 6F **19**
Linkadells PL7: P'ton 2E **20**
Linkadell Vs. PL7: P'ton 2E **20**
Linketty La. PL6: Ply 7E **12**
PL7: P'ton 3D **20**
Linketty La. E. PL6: Ply 6F **13**
Linketty La. W. PL3: Ply 1D **18** (not continuous)
Linnet Ct. PL12: Salt 5K **9**
Linton Cl. PL5: T Fol 6B **6**
Linton Rd. PL5: T Fol 6B **6**
Linton Sq. PL5: T Fol 6B **6**
Linton Wlk. PL5: T Fol 6B **6**
Lippell Dr. PL9: P'ock 3J **29**
LIPSON 1J 5 (5E 18)
Lipson Av. PL4: Ply 2K **5** (5F **19**)
Lipson Ct. PL4: Ply 2H **5** (5E **18**)
Lipson Hill PL4: Ply 1K **5** (5F **19**)
Lipson Rd. PL4: Ply 4F **19**
Lipson Sports Cen. 4G 19
Lipson St. PL4: Ply 4G **5** (6D **18**)
Lipson Ter. PL4: Ply 1K **5** (5F **19**)
LIPSON VALE 4F 19
Lipson Va. PL4: Ply 4F **19**
Lipstone Cres. PL4: Ply 1K **5** (5F **19**)
Liscawn Ter. PL11: Torp 5E **16**
Liskeard Rd. PL12: Nott, Salt, Trem 1D **8**
Lisson Gro. PL4: Ply 4D **18**
Lister Cl. PL7: P'ton 2G **21**
Litchaton Cres. PL7: P'ton 1C **20**
Litchaton Way PL7: P'ton 1C **20**
Litchfield Cl. PL7: P'ton 2J **21**
Lit. Ash Gdns. PL5: Ply 6E **10**
Lit. Ash Rd. PL5: Ply 6E **10**
Little Butts PL9: P'ock 3K **29**
Lit. Dock La. PL5: Ply 5K **11**
Lit. Down La. PL6: Rob 2J **7**
Lit. Fancy Cl. PL6: Ply 7H **7**
Little La. PL9: Stad 5J **29**
PL10: Kin *7D* ***26*** *(off Fore St.)*
Lit. Point Cres. PL10: Mill 4C **26**
Littleton Pl. PL2: Dev 4J **17**
Littlewood Cl. PL7: P'ton 4H **21**
Livingstone Av. PL8: Yeal 3K **35**
Lizard Cl. PL6: Ply 7E **6**
Lizard Wlk. PL6: Ply 7F **7**
Lockington Av. PL3: Ply 1E **18**
Locks Wlk. PL1: Dev 7H **17**
Lockyer Ct. PL1: Ply 6D **4**
Lockyer Rd. PL3: Ply 3D **18**
Lockyers Quay PL4: Ply 6H **5** (7E **18**)
Lockyer St. PL1: Ply 5D **4** (7C **18**) (not continuous)
Lockyer Ter. *PL12: Salt* *4D* ***10*** *(off Biscombe Gdns.)*
Lodge Gdns. PL6: Ply 4D **12**
Lodge La. PL8: Brix 4G **31**
Lofoten Cl. PL1: Dev 6H **17**
Loftus Gdns. PL5: Ply 5F **11**
Lollabury Rd. PL12: Salt 4B **10**
London Ct. PL21: Ivy 3E **24**
Long Acre PL12: Salt 3J **9**
Longacre PL7: P'ton 1C **20**
LONGBRIDGE 1K 19
Longbridge Av. PL6: Ply 2A **20**
Longbridge Cl. PL6: Ply 2A **20**
Longbridge Rd. PL6: Ply 1K **19**
Longbrook Barton PL7: P'ton 3E **20**
Longbrook Cl. PL21: Ivy 3B **24**
Longbrook Rd. PL21: Ivy 3C **24**
Longbrook St. PL7: P'ton 5G **21**
Longcause PL7: P'ton 4G **21**
Long Down Gdns. PL6: Ply 4K **13**
Longfield Pl. PL4: Ply 1H **5** (5E **18**)
Longfield Vs. PL9: P'ock 1J **29**
LONGLANDS 6G 9
Longlands La. PL12: Salt 6H **9**
Longlands Rd. PL9: P'ock 1J **29**
Long Ley PL3: Ply 2G **19**
Longmeadow PL7: P'ton 1E **20**
Longmeadow Cl. PL7: P'ton 1F **21**
Longmeadow Ct. PL12: Salt 4C **10**
Longmeadow Rd. PL12: Salt 4B **10**
Long Pk. Cl. PL9: P'ock 4A **30**
Long Pk. Dr. PL6: Ply 7J **7**
Long Pk. Rd. PL12: Salt 5A **10**
Longroom PL1: Ply 7A **4** (1A **28**)
Long Rowden PL3: Ply 2D **18**
Longstone Av. PL6: Ply 1F **13**
Long Ter. Cl. PL7: P'ton 3K **21**
Longview Rd. PL12: Salt 4A **10**
Longview Ter. PL3: Ply 2G **19**
Longwood Cl. PL7: P'ton 4H **21**
Lonsdale Vs. *PL4: Ply* *4E* ***18*** *(off Elm Rd.)*
Looe St. PL4: Ply 5F **5** (7D **18**)
Looseleigh Cl. PL6: Ply 3F **13**
Looseleigh La. PL6: Ply 2D **12**
Looseleigh Pk. PL6: Ply 2D **12**
Lopes Dr. PL6: Rob 5H **7**
Lopes Rd. PL2: Ply 2A **18**
Lopwell Cl. PL6: Ply 2E **12**
Lord Louis Cres. PL9: Hoo 3E **28**
Lord Robarts Ct. PL4: Ply 4J **5**
Lorrimore Av. PL2: Ply 3J **17**
Lotherton Cl. PL7: P'ton 5J **21**
Loughboro Rd. PL5: Ply 6F **11**
Love La. PL12: Salt 5B **10**
Lovell Rd. PL3: Ply 2E **18**
Lower Anderton PL10: Mill 4F **27**
Lwr. Anderton Rd. PL10: Mill 4C **26**
Lwr. Brook Pk. PL21: Ivy 3B **24**
LOWER COMPTON 3F 19
Lwr. Compton Rd. PL3: Ply 2E **18**
Lower Ct. Rd. PL8: N Fer 5E **34**
LOWER ERNESETTLE 2G 11
Lwr. Farm Rd. PL7: P'ton 4H **21**
Lwr. Fore St. PL12: Salt 5D **10**
Lower Pk. Dr. PL9: P'ock 5A **30**
Lwr. Port Vw. PL12: Salt 5C **10**
Lwr. Ridings PL7: P'ton 1J **21**
Lower Row PL10: Kin 7D **26**
Lwr. Saltram PL9: P'ock 2H **29**
Lowerside PL2: Ply 7J **11**
Lower St. PL4: Ply 5G **5** (7D **18**)
Lowertown Cl. PL12: Lan 1C **8**
Low Rd. PL9: Wem 3A **34**
Lucas La. PL7: P'ton 2E **20**
Lucas Ter. PL4: Ply 6G **19**
Ludlow Rd. PL3: Ply 2D **18**
Lulworth Dr. PL6: Ply 7G **7**
Lundy Cl. PL6: Ply 7E **6**
Luscombe Cl. PL21: Ivy 3B **24**
Luxmore Cl. PL6: Ply 6K **13**
Lych Cl. PL9: Hoo 3F **29**
Lydcot Wlk. PL6: Ply 7F **13**
Lydford Cl. PL21: Ivy 4E **24**
Lydford Pk. Rd. PL3: Ply 3C **18**
Lyd Gdns. PL19: Tav 3F **37**
Lydia Way PL4: Ply 1H **5** (5E **18**)
Lympne Av. PL5: Ply 2J **11**
Lyndhurst Cl. PL2: Ply 2B **18**
Lyndhurst Rd. PL2: Ply 2B **18**
Lyndon Ct. PL12: Salt 3A **10**
Lyndrick Rd. PL3: Ply 1D **18**
Lynher Ct. PL12: Salt 6C **10**
Lynher Dr. PL12: Salt 6B **10**
Lynher St. PL5: Ply 5G **11**
Lynmouth Cl. PL7: P'ton 1D **20**
Lynwood Av. PL7: P'ton 2B **20**

M

Macadam Rd. PL4: Ply 7K **5** (1F **29**)
Macandrew Wlk. PL21: Ivy 2F **25**
Macaulay Cres. PL5: Ply 6B **12**
Macey St. PL11: Torp 5E **16**
Mackenzie Pl. PL5: Ply 5F **11**
Madden Rd. PL1: Dev 6J **17**
Maddock Cl. PL7: P'ton 5H **21**
Maddock Dr. PL7: P'ton 4H **21**
Madeira Rd. PL1: Ply 7E **4** (1C **28**)
Madge Ct. *PL19: Tav* *2D* ***36*** *(off King St.)*
Madge La. PL19: Tav 3D **36**
Magdalen Gdns. PL7: P'ton 5G **21**
Magnolia Cl. PL7: P'ton 3J **21**
Magnolia Ct. *PL9: P'ock* *2A* ***30*** *(off Horn Cross Rd.)*
Maida Va. Ter. PL4: Ply 1H **5** (4E **18**)
Maidenwell Rd. PL7: P'ton 3D **20**
Maidstone Pl. PL5: Ply 3H **11**
Maine Gdns. PL2: Ply 1J **17**
MAINSTONE 4A 14
Mainstone Av. PL4: Ply 6K **5** (7F **19**)
Maitland Dr. PL3: Ply 7E **12**
Maker La. PL10: Mill 4C **26**
Maker Rd. PL11: Torp 6D **16**
Maker Vw. PL3: Ply 1A **4** (4A **18**)
Mallard Cl. PL7: P'ton 3G **21**
Mallet Rd. PL21: Ivy 2B **24**
Malmesbury Cl. PL2: Ply 7A **12**
Malory Cl. PL5: Ply 5C **12**
MANADON 6C 12
Manadon Cl. PL5: Ply 6D **12**

Manadon Dr.—Mt. Ford

Manadon Dr. PL5: Ply 6D 12
Manadon Football Development Cen. 5C 12
Manby Gdns. PL5: Ply 3J 11
Manifold Gdns. PL3: Ply 3J 19
MANNAMEAD 3F 19
Mannamead Av. PL3: Ply 3E 18
Mannamead Ct. *PL3: Ply 2E 18*
(off Lwr. Compton Rd.)
Mannamead Rd. PL3: Ply 7D 12
PL4: Ply 3D 18
Manor Cl. PL19: Tav 2C 36
PL21: Ivy 3D 24
Manor Ct. *PL3: Ply 3H 19*
(off Yeo Clo.)
PL3: Ply 2H 19
(Blandford Rd.)
Manor Dr. PL21: Ivy 3D 24
Manor Est. PL20: Hor 2A 38
Manor Gdns. PL10: Mill 3C 26
PL20: Hor 2A 38
Manor La. PL3: Ply 3J 19
Manor Pk. PL12: Salt 5A 10
Manor Pk. Cl. PL7: P'ton 3G 21
Manor Pk. Dr. PL7: P'ton 4G 21
Manor Rd. PL9: P'ock 1K 29
PL19: Tav 2D 36
Manor St. PL1: Ply 4A 4 (6A 18)
Manor Way PL21: Ivy 3D 24
Mansion, The PL21: Bit 6K 25
Manston Cl. PL5: Ply 2H 11
Mantle Gdns. PL5: Ply 7G 11
Maple Av. PL11: Torp 5D 16
Maple Cl. PL6: Ply 1K 13
PL19: Tav 5E 36
Maple Ct. PL9: P'ock 2A 30
Maple Gro. PL4: Ply 1E 4 (4C 18)
PL7: P'ton 3C 20
Maple Way PL6: Ply 7K 7
Mardon Cl. PL6: Ply 3J 13
Marett Rd. PL5: Ply 4J 11
Margaret Pk. PL3: Ply 7D 12
Marina Rd. PL5: Ply 4J 11
Marina Ter. PL4: Ply 1H 5 (4E 18)
Marine Cotts.
PL4: Ply 7J 5 (1E 28)
Marine Ct. PL11: Torp 6E 16
Marine Dr. PL11: Torp 6E 16
Marine Pl. PL4: Ply 7J 5 (1E 28)
Marine Rd. PL9: P'ock 2G 29
Mariners Ct. PL1: Ply 7K 17
PL4: Ply 5G 5
Maristow Av. PL2: Ply 3J 17
Maristow Cl. PL6: Ply 2E 12
Marjon Sports & Leisure 3G 13
Marjorie Kelly Way
PL21: Ivy 4D 24
Marjory Wlk. PL8: Yeal 6B 32
Market Av. PL1: Ply 4C 4 (6B 18)
Market Cl. PL1: Ply 7K 17
Market Rd. PL7: P'ton 3E 20
PL19: Tav 3E 36
Market Sq. PL1: Ply 4C 4 (6C 18)
Market Stalls
PL1: Ply 4C 4 (6B 18)
Market St. PL1: Ply 7K 17
(not continuous)
PL8: Yeal 5C 32
PL10: Kin 7D 26
PL19: Tav 2E 36
Market Way PL1: Ply 4C 4 (6B 18)
MARKWELL 6A 8
Markwell La. PL12: S Ern 6A 8
Marlborough Cl. PL12: Salt 6C 10
Marlborough Rd.
PL4: Ply 2F 5 (5D 18)
Marlborough Row PL1: Dev 6H 17
Marlborough St. PL1: Dev 6H 17
Marldon Cl. PL5: Ply 4A 12
Marlow Gdns. PL9: P'ock 4A 30
Marrowbone Slip
PL4: Ply 5H 5 (7E 18)
Marryat Gdns. PL5: Ply 6D 12
Marshall Cl. PL19: Whit 6F 37
Marshall Dr. PL21: Ivy 4D 24
Marshall Rd. PL7: P'ton 3B 20
PL19: Whit 6F 37
Marshals Fld. PL21: Ivy 3F 25
Marsh Cl. PL6: Ply 2A 20
MARSH MILLS 2B 20
Marsh Mills Junc. PL3: Ply 2A 20
Marsh Mills Pk. PL6: Ply 2A 20
Marsh Mills Retail Pk.
PL6: Ply 2A 20
Martin La. PL1: Ply 5B 4
PL4: Ply 5G 5
Martin St. PL1: Ply 5A 4 (7B 18)
Martlesham Pl. PL5: Ply 3J 11
Mary Dean Av. PL5: T Fol 7B 6
Mary Dean Cl. PL5: T Fol 7B 6
MARYFIELD 3B 16
Maryland Gdns. PL2: Ply 1J 17
Mary Seacole Rd.
PL1: Ply 4A 4 (6A 18)
Masefield Gdns. PL5: Ply 6A 12
Masterman Rd. PL2: Dev 4J 17
Maton Cl. PL21: Ivy 4E 24
Maudlins La. PL19: Tav 3C 36
Maunsell Cl. PL2: Ply 1J 17
Mavisdale PL2: Ply 2J 17
Maxwell Rd. PL4: Ply 1G 29
Maybank Rd.
PL4: Ply 3K 5 (6F 19)
Maybrook Dr. PL12: Salt 5A 10
Mayers Way PL9: Hoo 3J 29
Mayfair Cres. PL6: Ply 6G 13
Mayfair Ho. PL4: Ply 3G 5
Mayfield PL21: Ivy 4B 24
Mayflower Cl. PL9: P'ock 2A 30
Mayflower Dr. PL2: Ply 3A 18
Mayflower Intl. Marina
PL1: Dev 1J 27
Mayflower Leisure Cen. 3B 18
Mayflower Stone & Steps 7G 5
Mayflower St.
PL1: Ply 3D 4 (6C 18)
Mayflower Vis. Cen. 6F 5
Maynarde Cl. PL7: P'ton 3J 21
May Ter. PL4: Ply 3H 5 (6E 18)
Mead, The PL7: P'ton 1D 20
Mead Cl. PL21: Ivy 2B 24
Meadfoot Ter. PL4: Ply 3E 18
Meadow Brook PL19: Tav 4C 36
Meadow Cl. PL7: P'ton 4A 22
PL8: N Fer 4H 35
PL12: Salt 4C 10
Meadow Dr. PL8: Brix 5H 31
PL12: Salt 3A 10
Meadowfield Pl. PL7: P'ton 5J 21
Meadowlands PL6: Ply 7J 7
Meadowlands Leisure Pool
3D 36
Meadow Pk. PL9: Hoo 4H 29
Meadow Ri. PL7: P'ton 4H 21
Meadows, The PL11: Torp 4B 16
Meadowside PL9: P'ock 2A 30
Meadowsweet Pk.
PL12: Salt 5K 9
Meadow Vw. Rd.
PL7: P'ton 3D 20
Meadow Way PL7: P'ton 1E 20
Meadway PL12: Salt 6B 10
Meatherel Cl. PL21: Ivy 4C 24
Meavy Av. PL5: Ply 5D 12
Meavy Bourne PL20: Yel 6E 38
Meavy La. PL20: Yel 6D 38
Meavy Vs. PL20: Yel 6D 38
Meavy Way PL5: Ply 5D 12
PL19: Tav 3F 37
Medland Cres. PL6: Ply 1C 12
Medway Pl. PL3: Ply 2J 19
Megabowl
Barbican 6J 5 (7E 18)
Plympton 3C 20
Melbourne Cotts.
PL1: Ply 3B 4 (6B 18)
Melbourne Pl. PL1: Ply 2B 4
Melbourne St.
PL1: Ply 2B 4 (5B 18)
Melrose Av. PL2: Ply 7A 12
Melville Pl. *PL2: Ply 3K 17*
(off Melville Rd.)
Melville Rd. PL2: Ply 3K 17
Melville Ter. La. PL2: Ply 3K 17
MEMBLAND 5K 35
Memory La. PL9: P'ock 2K 29
Mena Pk. Cl. PL9: Elb 2C 30
Mena Pk. Rd. PL9: Elb 2C 30
Menhinick Cl. PL12: Lan 2C 8
Merafield Cl. PL7: P'ton 3C 20
Merafield Dr. PL7: P'ton 4D 20
Merafield Farm Cotts.
PL7: P'ton 4C 20
(off Merafield Rd.)
Merafield Ri. PL7: P'ton 4D 20
Merafield Rd. PL7: P'ton 4B 20
Mera Pk. PL12: Lan 2B 8
Merchant's House *5E 4*
(off Finewell St.)
Meredith Rd. PL2: Ply 1B 18
Merlin Cl. PL6: Ply 6J 7
Merrifield PL21: Filh 3H 25
Merrivale Rd. PL2: Ply 1K 17
PL5: Ply 4A 12
Mersey Cl. PL3: Ply 2J 19
Mews, The PL1: Ply 5J 17
PL11: Torp 6D 16
PL21: Bit 5K 25
Mewstone Av. PL9: Wem 4B 34
Michael Rd. PL3: Ply 3F 19
Michigan Way PL3: Ply 2H 19
Mid Churchway PL9: P'ock 2B 30
Middlecombe La.
PL8: N May 7G 35
Middle Down Cl.
PL9: P'ock 4B 30
Middlefield Cl. PL12: Salt 4J 9
Middlefield Rd. PL6: Ply 1C 12
Middle Leigh PL8: N Fer 5F 35
MIDDLEMOOR 6H 37
Middle Rd. PL9: Wem 3A 34
Middleton Wlk. PL5: Ply 3G 11
Midella Rd. PL20: Yel 6D 38
Miers Cl. PL5: Ply 7F 11
Milch Pk. PL12: Salt 5K 9
Mildmay St.
PL4: Ply 2G 5 (5D 18)
MILEHOUSE 4K 17
Milehouse Rd. PL3: Ply 4K 17
Miles Mitchell Av. PL6: Ply 6F 13
Milford La. PL5: Ply 2K 11
Military Rd. PL3: Ply 2J 19
PL6: Ply 1H 19
Milizac Cl. PL8: Yeal 5B 32
MILLBAY 7B 4 (7A 18)
Millbay Docks
PL1: Ply 7A 4 (1A 28)
Millbay Marina Village
PL1: Ply 7B 4 (1B 28)
Millbay Pk. 6B 4 (7B 18)
Millbay Rd. PL1: Ply 6A 4 (7A 18)
Mill Bri. PL1: Ply 5A 18
MILLBROOK 4B 26
Mill Cl. PL21: L Mil 4K 23
Miller Ct. PL1: Ply 5A 4 (7A 18)
Miller Way PL6: Ply 3H 13
MILLFIELDS, THE 6A 18
Mill Hill La. PL19: Tav 2A 36
Millhouse Pk. PL11: Torp 6D 16
Mill La. PL11: Torp 6D 16
Mill Leat Cl. PL8: Yeal 5D 32
Mill Mdw. PL21: Ivy 3E 24
MILL PARK 3B 10
Millpool Head PL10: Mill 4B 26
Millpool Rd. PL10: Mill 3C 26
Mill Rd. PL10: Mill 3C 26
Mills Rd. PL1: Dev 6J 17
Mill Vw. Gdns. PL10: Mill 4C 26
Mill Vw. Rd. PL10: Mill 4C 26
Millway Pl. PL9: P'ock 1J 29
Millwood Dr. PL6: Ply 6K 13
Milne Pl. PL1: Dev 5J 17
Milton Cl. PL5: Ply 5B 12
Milton Ct. PL4: Ply 7F 19
(not continuous)
Milton Cres. PL19: Tav 3F 37
Minerva Cl. PL7: P'ton 2H 21
Minses Cl. PL9: Elb 2D 30
Mirador Pl. PL4: Ply 5G 19
Misterton Cl. PL9: Elb 1C 30
Mitchell Cl. PL9: Hoo, P'ock 4J 29
Mitre Cl. PL19: Tav 5C 36
Modbury Cl. PL5: Ply 4A 12
Mohun's Cl. PL19: Tav 4E 36
Mohun's Pk. PL19: Tav 5E 36
Molesworth Cotts. *PL3: Ply 4K 17*
(off Molesworth Rd.)
Molesworth Rd. PL1: Ply 4K 17
PL3: Ply 4K 17
PL7: P'ton 2C 20
Molesworth Ter. PL10: Mill 4C 26
Mollison Rd. PL5: Ply 5H 11
Molyneaux Pl. PL1: Dev 5J 17
Moneycentre Precinct, The
PL1: Ply 3E 4 (6C 18)
Monica Wlk.
PL4: Ply 1H 5 (5E 18)
Monksmead PL19: Tav 4C 36
Monmouth Gdns. PL5: Ply 3B 12
Montacute Av. PL5: Ply 5K 11
Montgomery Cl. PL12: Salt 4A 10
PL21: Ivy 3F 25
Montpelier Rd. PL2: Ply 1B 18
Monument St. PL1: Dev 7H 17
Moon La. PL4: Ply 4G 5
Moon La. Flats *PL4: Ply 4G 5*
(off Moon La.)
Moon St. PL4: Ply 4G 5 (6D 18)
Moor Cotts. PL19: Whit 6H 37
Moorcroft Cl. PL9: P'ock 2B 30
Moorfield Av. PL6: Ply 1H 19
Moorfields PL21: Bit 6K 25
MOORHAVEN VILLAGE 5K 25
Moorland Av. PL7: P'ton 2F 21
Moorland Cl. PL21: Bit 6K 25
Moorland Ct. PL20: Yel 7B 38
Moorland Dr. PL7: P'ton 2F 21
Moorland Gdns. PL7: P'ton 2G 21
Moorland Rd. PL7: P'ton 3F 21
Moorlands Ind. Est.
PL12: Salt 3K 9
Moorlands La. PL12: Salt 3K 9
Moorland Vw. PL6: Ply 2F 13
PL9: Elb 2C 30
PL12: Salt 4C 10
Moor La. PL5: Ply 6H 11
Moor Pk. PL21: Bit 6K 25
Moor Vw. PL2: Ply 3J 17
PL3: Ply 4H 19
PL9: P'ock 2J 29
PL11: Torp 5E 16
Moorview Ct. PL6: Ply 2A 14
Moor Vw. Ter. PL4: Ply 4D 18
PL20: Yel 6D 38
Moreton Av. PL6: Ply 6E 12
Morgan Rd. PL6: Ply 1H 13
Morice Sq. PL1: Dev 6H 17
Morice St. PL1: Dev 6H 17
MORICE TOWN 4J 17
Morlaix Dr. PL6: Ply 3F 13
Morley Cl. PL7: P'ton 3B 20
Morley Ct. PL1: Ply 4C 4 (6B 18)
Morley Vw. Rd. PL7: P'ton 2D 20
Morrish Pk. PL9: P'ock 3A 30
Morshead Rd. PL6: Ply 5E 12
Mortain Rd. PL12: Salt 3A 10
Mortimore Cl. PL12: Salt 5A 10
Morwell Gdns. PL2: Ply 2K 17
Moses Cl. PL6: Ply 7D 6
Moses Ct. *PL6: Ply 7D 6*
(off Moses Clo.)
Mostyn Av. PL4: Ply 4F 19
Mote Pk. PL12: Salt 4K 9
Mothecombe Wlk. PL6: Ply 6K 13
Moulton Cl. PL7: P'ton 3J 21
Moulton Wlk. PL7: P'ton 4J 21
Mount Batten Cen., The 2E 28
Mt. Batten Cl. PL9: P'ock 3J 29
Mount Batten Sailing & Watersports Cen. 2E 28
Mt. Batten Way
PL9: P'ock 3J 29
Mount Edgcumbe Formal Gardens 2H 27
Mount Edgcumbe House 3F 27
Mount Edgcumbe Country Pk. 3J 27
Mt. Ford PL19: Tav 3C 36

Pearn Ridge PL3: Ply 1F **19**
Pearn Rd. PL3: Ply 1F **19**
Pearson Av. PL4: Ply 4E **18**
Pearson Rd. PL4: Ply 4E **18**
Peek La. PL21: Bit 1K **25**
Peeks Av. PL9: P'ock 2A **30**
Peel St. PL1: Ply 7K **17**
Peel St. Flats *PL1: Ply 6K 17*
(off Peel St.)
Pellew Pl. PL2: Dev 4J **17**
Pembrey Wlk. PL5: Ply 3H **11**
(not continuous)
Pembroke La. PL1: Dev 7H **17**
Pembroke St. PL1: Dev 7H **17**
(not continuous)
Pemros Rd. PL5: Ply 5E **10**
Pencair Av. PL11: Torp 6B **16**
Pencreber Rd. PL20: Hor 2B **38**
Pendeen Cl. PL6: Ply 1E **12**
Pendeen Cres. PL6: Ply 1E **12**
Pendennis Cl. PL3: Ply 7E **12**
PL11: Torp 5C **16**
Pendilly Av. PL11: Torp 6C **16**
Pengelly Cl. PL11: Wil 3C **16**
Pengelly Hill PL11: Wil 3C **16**
Pengelly Pk. PL11: Wil 3C **16**
Penlee Gdns. PL3: Ply 4K **17**
Penlee Pk. PL11: Torp 4B **16**
Penlee Pl. PL4: Ply 4E **18**
Penlee Rd. PL3: Ply 4K **17**
Penlee Way PL3: Ply . . .1A **4** (4K **17**)
Pennant Way PL21: L Mil 4K **23**
PENNTORR 5E 16
PENNYCOMEQUICK . . .1C 4 (5B 18)
Pennycomequick Hill
PL3: Ply 1C **4** (5B **18**)
Pennycomequick Vs.
PL4: Ply 1C **4**
PENNYCROSS 7C 12
Pennycross Cl. PL2: Ply 7C **12**
Pennycross Pk. Rd.
PL2: Ply 1B **18**
Penny's La. PL9: Elb 3E **30**
PENQUIT 7G 25
Penrith Cl. PL6: Ply 4J **13**
Penrith Gdns. PL6: Ply 4J **13**
Penrith Wlk. PL6: Ply 4J **13**
Penrose St. PL1: Ply . . .2C **4** (6B **18**)
Penrose Vs. PL4: Ply 4E **18**
Pentamar St. PL2: Dev 4H **17**
Pentillie Cres. PL4: Ply 4C **18**
Pentillie Rd. PL4: Ply 4D **18**
Pentire Rd. PL11: Torp 5C **16**
Pentland Cl. PL6: Ply 7E **6**
Pentyre Ter. PL4: Ply . . .2J **5** (5E **18**)
Pepper La. PL9: Elb 2E **30**
Pepper St. PL19: Tav 2E **36**
Pepys Pl. PL5: Ply 6C **12**
Perches Cl. PL8: Mem 5K **35**
Percy St. PL5: Ply 6G **11**
Percy Ter. PL4: Ply 4F **19**
Periwinkle Dr. PL7: P'ton 3K **21**
Perranporth Cl. PL5: Ply 4H **11**
Perryman Cl. PL7: P'ton 1F **21**
Peryn Rd. PL19: Tav 3C **36**
Peter Hopper's Hill
PL5: T Fol 1B **6**
PL6: Rob 1B **6**
Peter's Cl. PL9: Elb 2C **30**
Petersfield Cl. PL3: Ply 2G **19**
Peters Pk. Cl. PL5: Ply 6H **11**
Peter's Pk. La. PL5: Ply 5G **11**
Pethick Cl. PL6: Ply 1C **12**
Pethill Cl. PL6: Ply 5A **14**
PEVERELL 1C 18
Peverell Pk. Rd. PL3: Ply 1C **18**
Peverell Ter. PL3: Ply 3C **18**
Pew Tor Cl. PL19: Tav 3G **37**
PL20: Yel 5C **38**
Philip Cl. PL9: P'ock 3B **30**
Philip Gdns. PL9: P'ock 3A **30**
Phillimore St. PL2: Ply 4J **17**
Phoenix Cl. PL20: Hor 2B **38**
Phoenix St. PL1: Ply . . .5A **4** (7A **18**)
Pick Pie Dr. PL6: Ply 6K **7**
Pier St. PL1: Ply 7B **4** (1B **28**)
Pike Rd. PL3: Ply 3J **19**
Pilgrim Cl. PL2: Ply 2A **18**
Pilgrim Hall PL4: Ply 3F **5**
Pillar Wlk. PL6: Ply 7D **6**
Pill La. PL12: Salt 2B **10**
Pillmere Dr. PL12: Salt 3K **9**
Pillory Hill PL8: N May 6G **35**
Pinder Ct. PL19: Tav 3D **36**
Pinehurst Way PL21: Ivy 2B **24**
Pinewood Cl. PL7: P'ton 2G **21**
Pinewood Dr. PL6: Ply 7K **7**
Pinkham Ter. PL12: Car 1J **9**
Pin La. PL1: Ply 6F **5** (7D **18**)
Pinnacle Quay *PL4: Ply 7E 18*
(off Harbour Av.)
Pippins, The PL21: Ivy 3B **24**
PITT HILL 1D 24
Pixon La. PL19: Tav 4D **36**
Pixon Trad. Cen. PL19: Tav . . .4D **36**
Plaistow Cl. PL5: Ply 5H **11**
Plaistow Cres. PL5: Ply 5H **11**
Pleasure Hill PL9: P'ock 1A **30**
Pleasure Hill Cl. PL9: P'ock . . .1J **29**
Plintona Vw. PL7: P'ton 1F **21**
Plougastel Dr. PL12: Salt 4B **10**
Ploughboy M. PL12: Salt 4K **9**
Plough Grn. PL12: Salt 4K **9**
Ploughman Way PL8: Torr 6D **32**
Plover Ri. PL21: Ivy 3C **24**
Plumer Rd. PL6: Ply 5E **12**
Plybridge Rd. PL7: P'ton 5B **14**
Plymbridge Gdns.
PL7: P'ton 1D **20**
Plymbridge La. PL6: Ply 3G **13**
Plymbridge Rd. PL6: Ply 1H **13**
(Morgan Rd.)
PL6: Ply 6H **13**
(Novorossisk Rd., not continuous)
Plym Cres. PL19: Tav 3F **37**
PLYMOUTH 6D 18
Plymouth Argyle FC 3B 18
Plymouth Arts Cen. 5F 5
PLYMOUTH CITY AIRPORT . . .2H 13
Plymouth Dome 7D 4 (1C 28)
Plymouth International Bus. Pk.
PL6: Ply 4E **12**
PLYMOUTH NUFFIELD HOSPITAL,
THE 3G 13
Plymouth Pavilions . . .5B 4 (7B 18)
Plymouth Rd. PL3: Ply 3K **19**
PL6: Ply 2A **20**
PL7: P'ton 2B **20**
PL19: Tav, Whit 4D **36**
PL20: Hor 2B **38**
Plymouth Rd. Ind. Est.
PL19: Tav 5E **36**
Plymouth Ski Cen. 1K 19
Plymouth Station (Rail)
. . . . .1D **4** (5C **18**)
Plymouth Swallows School of
Gymnastics 3H 13
PLYMPTON 3F 21
Plympton By-Pass
PL7: P'ton 3B **20**
Plympton Castle 4F 21
Plympton Hill PL7: P'ton 5G **21**
PLYMPTON HOSPITAL 3E 20
PLYMPTON ST MAURICE 4G 21
Plympton Swimming Pool 3E 20
PLYMSTOCK 3K 29
Plymstock Rd. PL9: P'ock 2H **29**
Plym St. PL4: Ply 3G **5** (6D **18**)
Plymtree Dr. PL7: P'ton 1D **20**
Plym Valley Railway & Vis. Cen.
. . . . .1B 20
Pocklington Ri. PL7: P'ton 3F **21**
Pode Dr. PL7: P'ton 4J **21**
Point Cotts. PL9: Hoo 2G **29**
Poldrissick Hill PL12: Lan 4C **8**
Poldrissick La. PL12: Lan 2B **8**
Pollard Cl. PL9: Hoo 4G **29**
PL12: Salt 5J **9**
Pollards Way PL12: Salt 3B **10**
Polruan Ter.
PL1: Ply 3A **4** (6A **18**)
Polston Pk. PL9: Spr 5B **30**
Polzeath Gdns. PL2: Ply 7C **12**
POMPHLETT 1J 29
Pomphlett Cl. PL9: P'ock 1J **29**
(not continuous)
Pomphlett Farm Ind. Est.
PL9: P'ock 7K **19**
Pomphlett Gdns. PL9: P'ock . . .1J **29**
Pomphlett Rd. PL9: P'ock 1J **29**
Pondfield Rd. PL12: Salt 4J **9**
Ponsonby Rd.
PL3: Ply 1A **4** (4A **18**)
Poole Pk. Rd. PL5: Ply 7F **11**
Poplar Cl. PL7: P'ton 3J **21**
Popplestone Pk. PL8: Brix 4G **31**
Porsham Cl. PL6: Rob 5G **7**
Porsham La. PL5: T Fol 7C **6**
Porspoder Pl. PL10: Kin 7D **26**
Portal Pl. PL21: Ivy 3C **24**
Porteous Cl. PL1: Dev 5J **17**
Porter Way PL12: Salt 4K **9**
Portland Ct. PL1: Dev 5J **17**
Portland Pl. E.
PL4: Ply 2F **5** (5D **18**)
Portland Rd. PL1: Dev 5J **17**
Portland Sq.
PL4: Ply 3E **4** (5C **18**)
(not continuous)
Portland Sq. La. Nth.
PL4: Ply 2E **4** (5C **18**)
Portland Vs.
PL4: Ply 2E **4** (5C **18**)
Portreath Gdns. PL2: Ply 7C **12**
Portway Cl. PL9: Elb 2E **30**
PORTWORTHY 2H 15
Possession La. PL12: Lan 2C **8**
Potters Way PL7: P'ton 3E **20**
Pottery Est. PL10: Mill 3B **26**
Pottery Rd. PL1: Dev 5G **17**
Pottery Rd. Flats
PL1: Dev 5G **17**
Poultney Cl. PL7: P'ton 3H **21**
Pound Hill PL12: Lan 1B **8**
Pound Rd. PL20: B Mon 5A **38**
Pounds Pk. PL12: Salt 4C **10**
Pounds Pk. Rd. PL3: Ply 1C **18**
Pound St. PL1: Ply 1K **27**
Powderham Rd. PL3: Ply 1E **18**
Powis Gdns. PL5: Ply 5A **12**
Powisland Dr. PL6: Ply 2E **12**
Prestonbury Cl. PL6: Ply 7G **7**
Pridaux Cl. PL12: Salt 2K **9**
Prideaux Rd. PL21: Ivy 3F **25**
Pridham La. PL2: Ply 1C **18**
Priesthood Ter. PL10: Mill 4B **26**
Priestley Av. PL5: Ply 5H **11**
Primrose Cl. PL11: Torp 4B **16**
PL21: Ivy 3E **24**
Primrose Gdns. PL19: Tav 4G **37**
Primrose Mdw. PL21: Ivy 2B **24**
Primrose Wlk. PL12: Salt 3A **10**
Prince Maurice Ct.
PL4: Ply 4H **5** (6E **18**)
Prince Maurice Rd.
PL4: Ply 1J **5** (5E **18**)
Princes Rd. *PL6: Ply 1K 13*
(off Sycamore Way)
Princess Av. PL5: Ply 4K **11**
PL9: P'ock 3K **29**
Princess Cres. PL9: P'ock 3K **29**
Princess St.
PL1: Ply 5D **4** (7C **18**)
Princess Ter. Ope PL1: Ply 5E **4**
Princes St. PL1: Dev 6H **17**
Princess Way
PL1: Ply 5D **4** (7C **18**)
Priors Pk. PL9: P'ock 7B **20**
Priory Cl. PL19: Whit 5F **37**
PL21: Ivy 3C **24**
Priory Dr. PL7: P'ton 3E **20**
Priory Gdns. PL19: Whit 6F **37**
Priory Lawn Ter. PL3: Ply 2F **19**
Priory Mill PL7: P'ton 3E **20**
Priory Ridge PL7: P'ton 3E **20**
Priory Rd. PL3: Ply 2F **19**
Promenade, The
PL1: Ply 7C **4** (1B **28**)
Prospect La. PL12: Salt 4K **9**
Prospect Pl.
PL1: Ply 6B **4** (7B **18**)
Prospect Row PL1: Dev 7H **17**
Prospect Row Flats
PL1: Dev 7H 17
(off Prospect Row)
Prospect St.
PL4: Ply 3G **5** (6D **18**)
Prospect Ter. *PL10: Mill 4B 26*
(off Greenland)
Prospect Wlk. PL12: Salt 4K **9**
Prouse Cres. PL2: Ply 7B **12**
Prouse Ri. PL12: Salt 5B **10**
Providence Pl. PL1: Ply 5K **17**
Providence St.
PL4: Ply 2G **5** (5D **18**)
Prynne Cl. PL1: Ply 3C **4** (6B **18**)
Prysten House 5E 4
Pykes Down PL21: Ivy 4G **25**
Pym St. PL1: Dev 5J **17**
PL19: Tav 2E **36**
Pyne Vs. PL9: Hoo 3G **29**

Q

Quant Pk. PL19: Tav 2E **36**
Quarry Cotts. PL5: Ply 5A **12**
Quarry La. PL12: Lan 1C **8**
Quarry Pk. Av. PL9: P'ock 2J **29**
Quarry Pk. Rd. PL3: Ply 3C **18**
PL9: P'ock 2J **29**
Quarry St. PL11: Torp 5E **16**
Quarterdeck, The PL1: Ply 1K **27**
Quay, The PL9: P'ock 1H **29**
PL19: Tav 3D **36**
Quay La. PL12: Trem 6D **8**
Quay Rd. PL1: Ply 6F **5** (7D **18**)
Quayside PL19: Tav 3D **36**
Queen Alexandra Sq.
PL1: Ply 6A **18**
Queen Anne's Battery
PL4: Ply 7J **5** (1E **28**)
Queen Anne Ter. PL4: Ply 2F **5**
Queens Cl. PL6: Ply 1K **13**
Queen's Ga.
PL1: Ply 2A **4** (5A **18**)
PL4: Ply 1J **5** (5E **18**)
Queen's Ga. M.
PL4: Ply 1J **5** (5E **18**)
Queens Ga. Vs. PL4: Ply 1J **5**
Queen's Ga. Vs. Rd.
PL4: Ply 1J **5** (5E **18**)
Queens Rd. PL4: Ply . . .1J **5** (5E **18**)
PL5: Ply 4J **11**
Queen St. PL1: Dev 6G **17**
(not continuous)

R

Radcliffe Cl. PL6: Ply 1D **12**
Radford Av. PL4: Ply 7F **19**
Radford La. PL10: Mill 5A **26**
Radford Pk. Dr. PL9: P'ock 3J **29**
Radford Pk. Rd. PL9: P'ock . . .3J **29**
Radford Rd. PL1: Ply . . .7B **4** (1B **28**)
Radford Vw. PL9: P'ock 3J **29**
Radnor Hall PL4: Ply 3G **5**
Radnor Pl. PL4: Ply . . .3G **5** (6D **18**)
Radnor St. PL4: Ply . . .3G **5** (6D **18**)
RAF Memorial 7E 4 (1C 28)
Raglan Ct. *PL1: Dev 6J 17*
(off Damerel Cl.)
Raglan Gdns. PL1: Dev 6J **17**
Raglan Rd. PL1: Dev 6J **17**
Railway Cotts. PL2: Ply 3J **17**
PL19: Tav 2E **36**
Railway Vw. PL8: Brix 5F **31**
Raleigh Ct. PL7: P'ton 2J **21**
Raleigh Rd. PL21: Ivy 2B **24**
Raleigh St. PL1: Ply . . .4C **4** (6B **18**)
Ralph's Ct. PL19: Tav 3D **36**
Ramage Cl. PL6: Ply 4A **14**
Ramillies Av. PL5: Ply 3K **11**
Ramsey Gdns. PL5: Ply 6C **12**
Randwick Pk. Rd.
PL9: P'ock 2J **29**
Ransum Way PL19: Tav 4D **36**

St Stephen Rd.—Stonehouse Bri.

St Stephen Rd. PL7: P'ton 5G **21**
ST STEPHENS 6A 10
St Stephen's Hill PL12: Salt 6K **9**
St Stephen's Pl. PL7: P'ton . . .3F **21**
St Stephen's Rd. PL12: Salt . . .6A **10**
St Stephen St. PL1: Dev 7J **17**
St Teresa Ho. PL4: Ply 4G **5**
St Theresa's Ct. *PL1: Dev 6J 17*
(off Raglan Rd.)
St Thomas Cl. PL7: P'ton 5G **21**
St Thomas Ct. PL4: Ply 4G **5**
St Vincent St. PL2: Ply 4H **17**
St Werburgh Cl. PL9: Wem . . .4B **34**
Salamanca St. PL11: Torp 5E **16**
Salcombe Rd.
PL4: Ply 1J **5** (4E **18**)
Salisbury Ho. PL3: Ply 4A **18**
Salisbury Ope PL3: Ply 3A **18**
Salisbury Rd.
PL4: Ply 3H **5** (6E **18**)
SALTASH 5C 10
Saltash By-Pass PL12: Salt 3J **9**
Saltash Heritage Mus. & Local
History Study Cen. 5D 10
Saltash Ind. Est. PL12: Salt 3K **9**
Saltash Leisure Cen. 5B 10
Saltash Parkway Ind. Est.
PL12: Salt 3J **9**
Saltash Rd. PL2: Ply 3G **17**
PL3: Ply 1C **4** (5C **18**)
Saltash Station (Rail) 5D 10
Saltburn Rd. PL5: Ply 5F **11**
Saltmill Rd. PL12: Salt 3C **10**
Saltram Ho. PL7: P'ton 4A **20**
Saltram Ter. PL7: P'ton 3E **20**
Sampford Gdns. PL20: Hor 1D **38**
Sampford Ter. PL20: Hor 1C **38**
Sandford Rd. PL9: P'ock 1A **30**
Sandon Wlk. *PL6: Ply 7F 13*
Sand Quay La. *PL12: Salt 5D 10*
(off Elwell Rd.)
Sandy La. PL21: Ivy 3E **24**
Sandy Rd. PL7: P'ton 4K **21**
Sango Ct. PL10: Mill 3C **26**
Sango Rd. PL11: Torp 6D **16**
Sarum Cl. PL3: Ply 1E **18**
Saunders Wlk. PL6: Ply 1C **12**
Savage Rd. PL5: Ply 7F **11**
Savery Cl. PL21: Ivy 2F **25**
Savery Ter. PL4: Ply 4F **19**
Sawrey St. PL1: Ply 5A **4** (7A **18**)
School Cl. PL7: P'ton 1E **20**
PL19: Tav 3F **37**
School Dr. PL6: Ply 7J **7**
School La. PL7: P'ton 4F **21**
School Rd. PL12: Lan 1B **8**
PL19: Whit 6F **37**
Sconner Rd. PL11: Torp 5D **16**
Scott Av. PL5: Ply 7F **11**
Scott Bus. Pk. PL2: Ply 2K **17**
SCOTT HOSPITAL 2K 17
Scott Memorial 7J 17
Scott Rd. PL2: Ply 2K **17**
(Beacon Pk. Rd.)
PL2: Ply 3A **18**
(Outland Rd.)
Scotts Cotts *PL9: P'ock 1J 29*
(off Honcray)
Seacroft Rd. PL5: Ply 5F **11**
Seaton Av. PL4: Ply 4D **18**
Seaton Bus. Pk. PL6: Ply 4G **13**
Seaton La. PL4: Ply 4D **18**
Seaton Orchard PL7: S'ell 1D **22**
Seaton Pl. PL2: Ply 3J **17**
Seaton Swimming Pool 4F 13
Sea Vw. Av. PL4: Ply . . .1K **5** (5F **19**)
Sea Vw. Dr. PL9: Wem 3B **34**
Sea Vw. Ter. PL4: Ply . . .2J **5** (5E **18**)
Second Av. PL1: Dev 6K **17**
PL2: Ply 1H **17**
PL9: P'ock 7B **20**
Sedge Cl. PL21: Ivy 4E **24**
Sedley Way PL5: Ply 4C **12**
Sefton Av. PL4: Ply 4F **19**
Sefton Cl. PL4: Ply 5F **19**
Segrave Rd. PL2: Ply 3A **18**
Selkirk Pl. PL5: Ply 5D **12**
Sellon Ct. PL1: Ply 4C **4** (6B **18**)
Selsden Cl. PL9: Elb 3D **30**
Sendall's Way PL6: Ply 4E **12**
Sennen Cl. PL11: Torp 4C **16**
Sennen Pl. PL2: Dev 4H **17**
Serpell Cl. PL6: Ply 1D **12**
Seven Stars La. PL5: T Fol 1A **12**
Seven Trees Ct.
PL4: Ply 1G **5** (5E **18**)
Severn Pl. PL3: Ply 3H **19**
Seymour Av. PL4: Ply . . .2J **5** (5E **18**)
Seymour Dr. PL3: Ply 3E **18**
Seymour Ho. PL1: Dev 7J **17**
Seymour M. PL4: Ply . . .2K **5** (5F **19**)
Seymour Pk. PL3: Ply 3F **19**
Seymour Pl.
PL1: Ply 2A **4** (5A **18**)
Seymour Rd. PL3: Ply 3E **18**
PL7: P'ton 2C **20**
Seymour St.
PL4: Ply 3G **5** (6D **18**)
Shackleton Ct. PL5: Ply 6C **12**
Shaftesbury Cotts.
PL4: Ply 1G **5** (5D **18**)
Shaftesbury Ct.
PL4: Ply 2G **5** (5D **18**)
Shakespeare Rd. PL5: Ply 5A **12**
Shaldon Cres. PL5: Ply 4A **12**
Shallowford Cl. PL6: Ply 7H **13**
Shallowford Rd. PL6: Ply 1H **19**
Shapleys Gdns. PL9: P'ock . . .4B **30**
Shapters Rd.
PL4: Ply 6K **5** (7F **19**)
Sharon Way PL6: Ply 2F **13**
Sharrose Rd. PL9: Hoo 4G **29**
Shaw Way PL9: Hoo 2E **28**
Shearwood Cl. PL7: P'ton 2D **20**
Sheepstor Rd. PL6: Ply 6J **13**
Shell Cl. PL6: Ply 6K **13**
Shelley Av. PL19: Tav 3F **37**
Shelley Way PL5: Ply 6G **11**
Shepherds La.
PL4: Ply 5H **5** (7E **18**)
Sherborne Cl. PL9: Elb 3D **30**
Sherford Cres. PL5: Ply 4K **11**
PL9: Elb 2D **30**
Sherford Rd. PL9: Elb 2D **30**
Sherford Wlk. PL9: Elb 2F **31**
Sheridan Rd. PL5: Ply 6B **12**
Sherril Cl. PL9: P'ock 5A **30**
Sherwell Arc. PL4: Ply 2F **5**
Sherwell La.
PL4: Ply 2F **5** (5D **18**)
Sherwill Cl. PL21: Ivy 2B **24**
Shipley Wlk. PL6: Ply 6F **13**
Shirburn Rd. PL6: Ply 6G **13**
Shirley Gdns. PL5: Ply 6B **12**
Shoemaker's La.
PL12: Salt 5B **10**
Short Cotts. PL11: Torp 5D **16**
Short Pk. Rd. PL3: Ply 3C **18**
Shortwood Cres.
PL9: P'ock 2B **30**
Shrewsbury Rd. PL5: Ply 3A **12**
Shute Pk. Rd. PL9: P'ock 4A **30**
Sidmouth Cotts. PL4: Ply 1J **5**
Silver Birch Cl. PL6: Ply 7H **7**
Silver Stream Way
PL8: Brix 4J **31**
Silver St. PL12: Salt 5D **10**
Silver Ter. PL10: Mill 3D **26**
Simon Cl. PL9: P'ock 3K **29**
Sir John Hunt Sports Cen. . . .3C 12
Sithney St. PL5: Ply 6F **11**
Six O'Clock La. PL7: P'ton 4F **21**
Skardale Gdns. PL6: Ply 7J **13**
Skardon Pl. PL4: Ply . . .2F **5** (5D **18**)
Skerries Rd. PL6: Ply 7E **6**
Skylark Ri. PL6: Ply 6K **7**
Slade Cl. PL9: P'ock 4B **30**
Slatelands Cl. PL7: P'ton 5J **21**
Slipperstone Dr. PL21: Ivy 2B **24**
Smallack Cl. PL6: Ply 5E **12**
Smallack Dr. PL6: Ply 5E **12**
Smallridge Cl. PL9: P'ock 4A **30**
Smeaton Sq. PL3: Ply 2J **19**
Smeaton's Tower 7D 4 (1C 28)
SMITHALEIGH 5E 22
Smithaleigh Cvn. Pk.
PL7: Smi 5E **22**
Smithfield Dr. PL12: Salt 4J **9**
Smiths Way PL12: Salt 4J **9**
Smithy Cl. PL12: Salt 3K **9**
Snell Dr. PL12: Salt 4J **9**
Somerset Cotts. PL3: Ply 4K **17**
Somerset Pl. PL3: Ply 4K **17**
Somerset Pl. La.
PL3: Ply 4K **17**
Soper's Hill PL5: T Fol 5D **6**
Sortridge Pk. PL20: Hor 1A **38**
South Dartmoor Leisure Cen.
. . . . .3E 24
South Devon Tennis Cen. 4D 24
SOUTHDOWN 3E 26
Southdown Quay 3E 26
Sth. Down Rd. PL2: Ply 2A **18**
Southdown Rd. PL10: Mill 3C **26**
South Down Ter.
PL10: Mill 3D **26**
Southella Rd. PL20: Yel 6D **38**
Southern Cl. PL2: Ply 1J **17**
Southern Ter.
PL4: Ply 1H **5** (4E **18**)
Southernway PL9: P'ock 2B **30**
Southfield PL12: Salt 5K **9**
Southgate Av. PL9: P'ock 4K **29**
Southgate Cl. PL9: P'ock 4K **29**
South Hill PL1: Ply 5K **17**
PL9: Hoo 4H **29**
Southland Pk. Cres.
PL9: Wem 3B **34**
Southland Pk. Rd.
PL9: Wem 4B **34**
Sth. Milton St.
PL4: Ply 6K **5** (7F **19**)
SOUTH PILL 3B 10
Southside Ope PL1: Ply 6F **5**
Southside St.
PL1: Ply 6F **5** (7D **18**)
South Vw. PL5: Ply 5D **12**
PL7: Hem 1K **21**
PL9: Elb 3C **30**
PL20: Hor 2B **38**
Southview PL10: Mill 3D **26**
South Vw. Cl. PL7: P'ton 1E **20**
South Vw. Pk. PL7: P'ton 1E **20**
South Vw. Ter.
PL4: Ply 3K **5** (6F **19**)
SOUTHWAY 1F 13
Southway Dr. PL6: Ply 2C **12**
(not continuous)
Southway La. PL6: Ply 1B **12**
(Coombe La.)
PL6: Ply 7G **7**
(Lulworth Dr.)
Southwell Rd. PL6: Ply 7D **12**
Sovereign Ct. PL7: P'ton 3D **20**
Sparke Cl. PL7: P'ton 4J **21**
Speakers Rd. PL21: Ivy 3F **25**
Speares, The PL12: Salt 5J **9**
Speculation Cotts.
PL8: Yeal 5B **32**
Speedwell Cl. PL10: Mill 4C **26**
Speedwell Cres. PL6: Ply 1F **19**
Speedwell Wlk. PL6: Ply 1G **19**
Spencer Gdns. PL12: Salt 6B **10**
Spencer Rd. PL9: P'ock 1K **29**
Spinnaker Quay PL9: Hoo 2E **28**
Spinney, The PL7: P'ton 4H **21**
PL21: Ivy 3B **24**
Spire Ct. PL3: Ply 2G **19**
Spire Hill Pk. PL12: Salt 5K **9**
SPRIDDLESTONE 5E 30
Springfield PL20: Hor 2C **38**
Springfield Av. PL9: Elb 3C **30**
Springfield Cl. PL9: Elb 3C **30**
Springfield Dr. PL3: Ply 4K **17**
Springfield La. PL9: Elb 2C **30**
Springfield Ri. PL9: Elb 2C **30**
Springfield Rd. PL9: Elb 3B **30**
Spring Hill PL19: Tav 3D **36**
Springhill PL2: Ply 7B **12**
Springhill Grn. PL2: Ply 7B **12**
Spring Pk. PL6: Ply 7K **7**
Springwood Cl. *PL7: P'ton 5H 21*
(off Wolverwood La.)
PL7: P'ton 5H **21**
(Cherry Pk.)
PL21: Ivy 3F **25**
Spruce Gdns. PL7: P'ton 3J **21**
Sprys Tenements PL20: Hor . . .1B **38**
Square, The PL1: Ply 6K **17**
PL10: Kin 7D **26**
PL12: Salt 4K **9**
Stable Cotts. PL7: P'ton 3F **21**
STADDISCOMBE 6K 29
Staddiscombe Rd.
PL9: P'ock, Stad 6K **29**
Staddon Cres. PL9: P'ock 3K **29**
Staddon Grn. PL9: P'ock 3J **29**
Staddon La. PL9: Bov 5G **29**
Staddon Pk. Rd. PL9: P'ock . . .4K **29**
Staddon Ter. La.
PL1: Ply 2C **4** (5B **18**)
Stag La. PL9: Elb 1C **30**
Stamford Cl. PL9: Hoo 3F **29**
Stamford Fort Cotts.
PL9: Hoo 3F 29
(off Stamford Rd.)
Stamford La. PL9: Hoo 4F **29**
Stamford Rd. PL9: Hoo 3F **29**
Stamps Hill PL8: Brix 3H **31**
Stanborough Cross
PL9: Elb 2D **30**
Stanborough Rd.
PL9: Elb, P'ock 2A **30**
Stanbury Av. PL6: Ply 6E **12**
Standarhay Cl. PL9: Elb 2D **30**
Standarhay Vs. PL9: Elb 2D **30**
Stangray Av. PL4: Ply 4C **18**
Stanhope Rd. PL5: Ply 5F **11**
Staniforth Dr. PL21: Ivy 4E **24**
Stanlake Cl. PL12: Salt 5A **10**
Stanley Pl. PL4: Ply 6G **19**
Stannary Bri. Rd. PL19: Tav . . .2F **37**
Stannary Cl. PL21: Ivy 3F **25**
Stannary Ct. *PL19: Tav 3D 36*
(off Garden La.)
Staple Cl. PL6: Rob 5H **7**
Stapleford Gdns. PL5: Ply 2J **11**
Station Rd. PL2: Ply 3H **17**
PL5: T Fol 1H **11**
PL7: P'ton 2F **21**
PL9: Elb 2D **30**
PL12: Salt 5D **10**
PL20: Hor 2B **38**
PL21: Ivy 2E **24**
Steeple Cl. PL9: P'ock 5A **30**
Steer Pk. Rd. PL7: P'ton 3K **21**
Steer Point Cotts. PL8: Brix . . .7G **31**
Steer Point Rd. PL8: Brix 5H **31**
Stefan Cl. PL9: Hoo 4G **29**
Stenlake Pl. *PL4: Ply 6G 19*
(off Stenlake Ter.)
Stenlake Ter. PL4: Ply 6G **19**
Stentaway Cl. PL9: P'ock 1A **30**
Stentaway Dr. PL9: P'ock 1A **30**
Stentaway Rd. PL9: P'ock 2A **30**
Stephenson Way PL5: Ply 5J **11**
Stibb La. PL21: Ivy 2A **24**
Stillman Ct. PL4: Ply 5F **5**
Stillman St. PL4: Ply . . .5F **5** (7D **18**)
Stirling Ct. PL5: Ply 6F **11**
Stirling Rd. PL5: Ply 6F **11**
Stoggy La. PL7: P'ton 2G **21**
(not continuous)
STOKE 1A 4 (5K 17)
Stoke Damerel Community
Sports Cen 4A 18
Stoke Rd. PL1: Ply 3A **4** (6A **18**)
PL8: N May 6G **35**
Stokesay Av. PL6: Ply 2E **12**
Stokes La. PL1: Ply 6F **5**
Stokingway Cl. PL9: P'ock 4K **29**
Stone Barton Cl. PL7: P'ton . . .2D **20**
Stone Barton Rd.
PL7: P'ton 2D **20**
Stonehall Flats PL1: Ply 7K **17**
Stonehedge Cl. PL21: Ivy 4E **24**
STONEHOUSE 7K 17
Stonehouse Bri. PL1: Ply 7K **17**

Uplands PL12: Salt 6B 10	Voss Rd. PL12: Salt, Trem 2F 9
Up. . . . PL19: Tav 4C 36	Vue Cinema
Up. Knollys Ter. La.	Plymouth 6J 5 (7E 18)
PL3: Ply 1B 4 (4B 18)	
Up. Ridings PL7: P'ton 1J 21	**W**
Upperton La. PL6: Rob 2K 7	
Upton Cl. PL3: Ply 1G 19	Waddon Cl. PL7: P'ton 1F 21
Uxbridge Dr. PL5: Ply 3H 11	Wadham Ter. PL2: Ply 3K 17

V

Vaagso Cl. PL1: Dev 6H 17
Valiant Av. PL5: Ply 3K 11
Valletort Cotts. PL1: Ply . . .5K 17
Valletort Flats *PL1: Ply* 6K 17
  (off Valletort Pl.)
Valletort Ho. PL1: Ply 2C 4
  PL1: Ply 5A 4 (7A 18)
  (Union St.)
Valletort La. PL1: Ply 5K 17
Valletort Pl. PL1: Ply 6K 17
Valletort Rd. PL1: Ply 5K 17
Valletort Ter. *PL1: Ply* 5A 18
  (off Valletort Rd.)
Valley Dr. PL9: Wem 3B 34
Valley Rd. PL7: P'ton 3C 20
  PL12: Salt 5B 10
Valley Vw. PL6: Ply 7J 7
Valley Vw. Cl. PL3: Ply 1G 19
Valley Vw. Rd. PL3: Ply 1G 19
Valley Wlk. PL6: Ply 1J 13
Vanguard Cl. PL5: Ply 6C 12
Vapron Rd. PL3: Ply 2D 18
Vauban Pl. PL2: Dev 4J 17
Vaughan Cl. PL2: Ply 1B 18
Vauxhall Ct. PL4: Ply 5F 5
Vauxhall Quay
  PL4: Ply 5G 5 (7D 18)
Vauxhall St. PL1: Ply . . .6F 5 (7D 18)
Vauxhall St. Flats PL4: Ply 5G 5
Veasy Pk. PL9: Wem 3C 34
Venn Cl. PL3: Ply 2D 18
Venn Ct. PL3: Ply 2D 18
  PL8: Brix 5H 31
Venn Cres. PL3: Ply 2D 18
Venn Dr. PL8: Brix 5H 31
Venn Gdns. PL3: Ply 1D 18
Venn Gro. PL3: Ply 1D 18
Venn La. PL3: Ply 2B 18
Venn Way PL3: Ply 1D 18
VENTON 2F 23
Vermont Gdns. PL2: Ply 1J 17
Verna Pl. PL5: Ply 5G 11
Verna Rd. PL5: Ply 5G 11
Vicarage Gdns. PL5: Ply 5E 10
Vicarage Hill PL8: Holb 7K 33
Vicarage Rd. PL7: P'ton 3D 20
  PL11: Torp 6E 16
Victoria Av. PL1: Ply . . .2A 4 (5A 18)
Victoria Cotts. PL6: Ply 7G 13
  PL12: Salt 4B 10
Victoria La. PL12: Salt 5C 10
Victoria Pk. PL1: Ply . . .2A 4 (5A 18)
Victoria Pl. *PL1: Ply* 7A 18
  (off Millbay Rd.)
  PL2: Dev 4J 17
Victoria Rd. PL5: Ply 6G 11
  PL12: Salt 5C 10
Victoria St. PL11: Torp 5E 16
Victoria Ter. PL4: Ply . . .1E 4 (5D 18)
Victoria Wharf PL4: Ply 7J 5
Victory St. PL2: Ply 2H 17
Vigo Bri. Rd. PL19: Tav 2E 36
Vigo M. PL19: Tav 2E 36
Village Dr. PL6: Rob 5H 7
Villiers Cl. PL9: P'ock 2J 29
Vincent Way PL12: Salt 5C 10
Vine Cres. PL2: Ply 2A 18
Vine Gdns. PL2: Ply 2A 18
Vinery La. PL7: P'ton 2E 30
  PL9: Elb 2E 30
Vinstone Way PL5: Ply 6G 11
Violet Dr. PL6: Ply 6K 7
Violet La. PL19: Tav 3F 37
Virginia Gdns. PL2: Ply 1J 17
Vixen Tor Cl. PL20: Yel 5C 38

Waggon Hill PL7: P'ton 4H 21
Wain Pk. PL7: P'ton 4G 21
Wakefield Av. PL5: Ply 6H 11
Wake St. PL4: Ply 1C 4 (5B 18)
Walcot Cl. PL6: Ply 4K 13
Waldon Cl. PL7: P'ton 2J 21
Walker Ter. PL1: Ply 7B 4 (1B 28)
Walkham Bus. Pk. PL5: Ply 6A 12
Walkham Cl. PL19: Tav 3F 37
Walkham Mdws. PL20: Hor . . .2C 38
Walkhampton Rd.
  PL20: Hor 2B 38
Walkhampton Wlk. PL6: Ply . . .6K 13
Walkham Ter. PL20: Hor 1B 38
Walkham Vw. PL20: Hor 2B 38
Wallace Rd. PL7: P'ton 4H 21
Wallpark Cl. PL7: P'ton 1G 21
Wardlow Cl. PL6: Ply 7E 12
Wardlow Gdns. PL6: Ply 7E 12
Wardour Wlk. PL6: Ply 7G 7
  (not continuous)
Ward Pl. PL3: Ply 3G 19
Warfelton Cres. PL12: Salt . . .5B 10
Warfelton Gdns. PL12: Salt . . .5B 10
Warfelton Ter. *PL12: Salt* 5B 10
  (off Windsor La.)
Waring Rd. PL6: Ply 7C 6
Warleigh Av. PL2: Ply 3H 17
Warleigh Cres. PL6: Ply 2E 12
Warleigh La. PL2: Ply 3H 17
Warleigh Point Nature Reserve
  . . . . .1G 11
Warleigh Rd. PL4: Ply 3H 17
Warleigh Vs. *PL12: Salt* 5D 10
  (off Culver Rd.)
Warmwell Rd. PL5: Ply 3H 11
Warran La. PL19: Tav 5E 36
Warraton Cl. PL12: Salt 4A 10
Warraton Grn. *PL12: Salt* 4A 10
  (off Warraton La.)
Warraton La. PL12: Salt 4A 10
Warraton Rd. PL12: Salt 4A 10
Warren Cl. PL9: Wem 4A 34
Warren La. PL9: Wem 4D 34
  PL21: Ivy 5J 23
Warren Pk. PL6: Ply 7J 7
Warren St. PL2: Dev 4H 17
Warspite Gdns. PL5: Ply 5C 12
Warwick Av. PL5: Ply 3C 12
Warwick Orchard Cl.
  PL5: Ply 4A 12
Wasdale Cl. PL6: Ply 5J 13
Wasdale Gdns. PL6: Ply 5J 13
Washbourne Cl. PL1: Dev 5H 17
Waterloo Ct. PL1: Ply 6K 17
Waterloo St. PL1: Ply 6K 17
  PL4: Ply 2G 5 (5D 18)
Waterloo Yd. Flats PL1: Ply . . .6K 17
Waterside Ho. PL1: Ply 4D 24
Waterside Row *PL21: Ivy* 4D 24
  (off Keaton Rd.)

Waterslade Dr. PL21: Ivy 4F 25
Watery La. PL6: Rob 1C 6
Watson Gdns.
  PL4: Ply 4J 5 (6E 18)
Watson Pl. PL4: Ply 4K 5 (6E 19)
Watts Pk. Rd. PL2: Ply 1B 18
Watts Rd. PL4: Ply 3K 5 (6E 19)
  PL19: Tav 3D 36
Waveney Gdns. PL5: Ply 4B 12
Waverley Rd. PL5: Ply 5G 11
Wavish Pk. PL11: Torp 5B 16
Waycott Wlk. PL6: Ply 1B 12
Wayside PL21: Ivy 3D 24
WEARDE 6C 10
Wearde Rd. PL12: Salt 5A 10
Weatherdon Dr. PL21: Ivy 3G 25
Weir Cl. PL6: Ply 5A 14
Weir Gdns. PL6: Ply 5A 14
Weir Rd. PL6: Ply 4K 13
Welbeck Av. PL4: Ply . . .1E 4 (5C 18)
Welland Gdns. PL3: Ply 3H 19
Wellfield Cl. PL7: P'ton 3K 21
Well Gdns. PL1: Ply . . .3C 4 (6B 18)
Wellhay Cl. PL9: Elb 3D 30
Wellington St. PL1: Ply 5K 17
  PL4: Ply 2G 5 (5D 18)
  PL11: Torp 5E 16
Well Pk. Rd. PL11: Torp 5E 16
Wellsbourne Pk. PL3: Ply 2F 19
Wells Cl. PL10: Mill 5B 26
Wellstones Cl. PL21: Ivy 4F 25
Welman Rd. PL10: Mill 3C 26
Welsford Av. PL3: Ply 3J 17
WEMBURY 3B 34
Wembury Marine Cen. 5A 34
Wembury Mdw. PL9: Wem 2C 34
Wembury Pk. Rd. PL3: Ply . . .2C 18
Wembury Rd.
  PL9: Elb, Spr, Wem 4B 30
Wenlock Gdns. PL2: Ply 7A 12
Wensum Cl. PL7: P'ton 4H 21
Wentwood Gdns. PL6: Ply . . .4K 13
Wentwood Pl. PL6: Ply 4K 13
Wentworth Pl. PL4: Ply 6G 19
Wentworth Way PL12: Salt . . .5K 9
Wesley Av. PL3: Ply 3D 18
Wesley Ct. PL1: Ply 6C 4
  PL11: Torp 5F 17
  (off King St.)
Wesley La. PL12: Salt 5C 10
Wesley Pl. PL2: Dev 4K 17
  PL3: Ply 3D 18
Wesley Rd. PL12: Salt 5C 10
Wesley Ter. PL12: Lan 2B 8
West Av. PL19: Tav 3D 36
Westbourne Rd. PL3: Ply 3C 18
Westbourne Ter. PL12: Salt . . .4C 10
Westbridge Cotts.
  PL19: Tav 4D 36
Westbridge Ind. Est.
  PL19: Tav 4D 36
Westbury Cl. PL5: Ply 3A 12
Westcombe Cres. PL9: Hoo . . .4J 29
Westcott Cl. PL6: Ply 7F 13
Westcountry Cl. PL2: Ply 1J 17
Westcroft Rd. PL5: Ply 6G 11
W. Devon Bus. Pk.
  PL19: Tav 5D 36
W. Down Rd. PL2: Ply 2A 18
Westella Rd. PL20: Yel 6D 38
W. End Ter. PL10: Mill 5B 26
Westeria Ter. PL2: Ply 1B 18
Western App.
  PL1: Ply 4C 4 (6B 18)
Western College Rd.
  PL4: Ply 3E 18
Western Dr. PL3: Ply 4G 19
Western Rd. PL21: Ivy 4D 24
Western Wood Way
  PL7: P'ton 3A 22
Westfield PL7: P'ton 2G 21
Westfield Av. PL9: Hoo 3H 29
W. Hill Rd. PL4: Ply 1J 5 (4E 18)
W. Hoe Rd. PL1: Ply . . .6B 4 (7B 18)
Westlake Cl. PL11: Torp 5C 16

West La. PL12: Lan 1A 8
W. Malling Av. PL5: Ply 2H 11
Westmoor Cl. PL7: P'ton 2K 21
Westmoor Pk. PL19: Tav 4E 36
WESTON MILL 7J 11
Weston Mill Crematorium
  PL2: Ply 1J 17
Weston Mill Dr. PL5: Ply 1H 17
Weston Mill Hill PL5: Ply 6H 11
Weston Mill La. PL5: Ply 6K 11
Weston Mill Rd. PL5: Ply 6H 11
Westover Cl. PL21: Ivy 3C 24
Westover Ind. Est.
  PL21: Ivy 4C 24
Westover La. PL21: Ivy 4C 24
WEST PARK 4K 11
West Pk. Dr. PL7: P'ton 3K 21
West Pk. Hill PL7: P'ton 1J 21
Westpark Vs. PL20: Hor 1B 38
West Quay *PL10: Mill* 4B 26
  (off Dawes La.)
West St. PL10: Mill 5B 2
  PL19: Tav 3D 36
West Vw. PL19: Whit 6G 37
Westway PL9: Hoo 4G 29
WEST WEMBURY 2C 34
Westwood Av. PL6: Ply 1H 13
Wharf, The PL19: Tav 3E 36
Wheatridge PL7: P'ton 1C 20
Whimple St.
  PL1: Ply 5E 4 (7D 18)
Whin Bank Rd. PL5: Ply 5C 12
Whistley Down PL20: Yel 6A 38
Whitby Cres. PL6: Ply 6F 13
Whitby Rd. PL6: Ply 6F 13
WHITCHURCH 6G 37
Whitchurch Rd.
  PL19: Tav, Whit 4E 36
  PL20: Hor 1B 38
White Cross Ct. PL4: Ply 3G 5
Whitefield Ter.
  PL4: Ply 2H 5 (5E 18)
Whiteford Rd. PL3: Ply 2D 18
Whiteford Rd. La. Sth.
  PL3: Ply 3D 18
White Friars La.
  PL4: Ply 4H 5 (6E 18)
Whitehall Dr. PL9: Elb 2C 30
White Lady Rd.
  PL9: Hoo, P'ock 4J 29
White La. PL1: Ply 6F 5
Whitewater Ct. PL7: P'ton . . .2E 20
Witham Pk. PL19: Tav 4E 36
WHITLEIGH 3B 12
Whitleigh Av. PL5: Ply 5D 12
Whitleigh Cotts. *PL5: Ply* 5D 12
  (off Whitleigh Av.)
Whitleigh Ct. PL5: Ply 3C 12
Whitleigh Grn. PL5: Ply 3B 12
Whitleigh Vs. PL5: Ply 5D 12
Whitleigh Way PL5: Ply 4B 12
  (not continuous)
Whitsoncross La. PL5: T Fol . . .7B 6
Whittington St.
  PL3: Ply 1A 4 (5A 18)
Widdicombe Dr. PL21: Ivy 4E 24
WIDEWELL 7G 7
Widewell La. PL6: Ply 7H 7
Widewell Rd. PL6: Ply 1G 13
Widey Ct. PL6: Ply 6E 12
Widey Hill PL8: N Fer 5J 35
Widey La. PL6: Ply 6E 12
Widey Vw. PL3: Ply 2E 18
WILCOVE 2C 16
Wilcove La. PL11: Wil 3B 16
Wilderness Rd. PL3: Ply 3D 18
Wilkinson Rd. PL5: Ply 7F 11
William Evans Cl. PL6: Ply . . .2C 12
William Prance Rd.
  PL6: Ply 4F 13
Williams Av. PL4: Ply 7G 19
Willowby Gdns. PL20: Yel 6D 38
Willowby Pk. PL20: Yel 6D 38
Willow Cl. PL7: P'ton 3E 20
Willow Cotts. PL7: P'ton 3E 20
Willow Ct. PL6: Ply 1K 19

STOP → 83001